MODULAR COURSES IN TECHNOLOGY
PNEUMATICS

Teacher's Guide

Peter Patient

Roy Pickup

Norman Powell

Oliver & Boyd

in association with the National Centre for School Technology

PROJECT TEAM

Director
Dr Ray Page

Co-ordinators
Roy Pickup
John Poole

Jeffrey Hall
Dr Duncan Harris
John Hucker
Michael Ive
Peter Patient

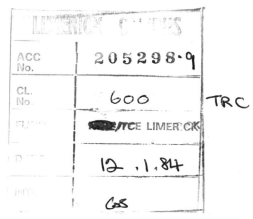
Oliver & Boyd
Robert Stevenson House
1–3 Baxter's Place
Leith Walk
Edinburgh EH1 3BB

A Division of Longman Group Ltd

ISBN 0 05 003536 3

First published 1983

Printed in Hong Kong
by Hing Yip Printing Co

Contents

Preface

This module is one of fourteen developed by the Schools Council Modular Courses in Technology Project, and can be used for existing courses in science, applied science, technology, technical studies, craft and design. It can also be used to build a modular course in technology, two examples of which have been tested by the Project.

The Southern Universities Joint Board and the South Western Examinations Board examine at O and CSE level respectively a scheme based on a common core of three modules (*Energy Resources, Materials Technology* and *Problem Solving*), a choice of two further modules and a major one-term project. Each module then occupies approximately ten weeks of four 35-minute periods a week.

The second scheme meets the syllabus requirements for the Cambridge University Board at O level and the East Anglian Board at CSE; it involves the use of three modules and a major two-term project, with background teaching about energy resources, the social implications of technological development, and technological problem solving. This scheme is based on modules providing for twelve weeks of four 35-minute periods a week.

This particular module is designed for a twelve-week programme which, if it is used for the first scheme, can be reduced to ten weeks by limiting the optional work.

While designed to service the needs of O-level and CSE courses, this module also covers a substantial part of the theoretical work in the Pneumatic Mechanisation section of the Automation module in the Cambridge A-level Technology syllabus.

Further details about using the 'Modular Courses in Technology' material and the two modular technology schemes that have been developed and tested by the Project can be obtained from the Teacher's Master Manual which is published by the National Centre for School Technology in association with Oliver & Boyd.

1 Teaching the Pneumatics Module

This module introduces pupils to a field of technology which is of immense importance in industry for the automation and control of manufacturing processes. Pupils find pneumatics a demanding but stimulating study, while the availability of industrial equipment for practical work gives the added satisfaction of being involved with 'the real thing'. In the course, pupils learn about basic pneumatic devices and simple pneumatic control systems and their applications. While this is good in itself, a special strength of the module is the scope it gives for design work. Chapter 12 of the pupil text and Activity 12 give an indication of, but by no means exhaust, this possibility. A further attribute is that pneumatic components and systems are analogous to those of other fields of technology, especially electronics. A prior study of pneumatics enables pupils to cope much more easily with the more abstract and less tangible nature of electronics. Beyond the module itself and in the realm of examination project work, pneumatics has a special value. It is a simple, convenient and compact way of providing a project with sufficient 'muscle' to make it work effectively, while its control and sensing systems, especially those described in Chapters 10 and 11 of the pupil text which use a low pressure air supply, provide valuable alternatives to the ubiquitous electronic-based control and sensing systems. However, while in no way devaluing this latter point, it is the case that pneumatic systems easily interface with electronic/microelectronic systems. A marriage of the two opens up to schools exciting possibilities in computer controlled robotics and automation.

The course is a mixture of basic material, denoted by the symbol '■', and more advanced material, denoted by the symbol '□'. The basic material will enable average ability pupils to cover the pneumatics content of most CSE technology syllabuses. The more advanced sections develop naturally from the basic material and are intended for more able pupils, enabling them to expand their knowledge, consider more complex examples, carry out calculations and suggest and evaluate designs. Pupils working through these sections will cover the pneumatics content of most O-level technology syllabuses.

The course contains a considerable amount of work even for top O-level pupils. It is intended that teachers are selective in the use of the material in a manner dictated by their circumstances. The pupil text can be used as a basis for theory lessons. It can be used as background reading to fill out a teacher's self-devised theory lessons. Portions could be set for homework reading together with questions requiring written answers which can only be completed by reading the text. For able pupils, the text could be the source from which they compile their own set of course notes. The essential companion to the text is the practical work detailed in the Workbook. This work demands much more than a slavish following of a circuit diagram. It is essential that there be an understanding of what is going on in a circuit along with 'why' and 'how'. Equally important is a growing ability to recognise, diagnose and rectify faults in a circuit which does not function as planned. A practical work notebook should be kept and full details of all work logged, including circuit diagrams. By this means pupils will become fluent in the use of pneumatic symbols, and in the designing and interpretation of circuits.

At each stage of the course the teacher must devise and set, as homework or classwork, design problems whose solution requires much more than rote redrawing of a pneumatic circuit from the course text. Such problems complement and give point to the handling of equipment and the piping up of standard circuits. Moreover, they give essential experience in design and problem solving prior to the tackling of examination projects.

The pneumatics course is intended to last twelve weeks but can be shortened to ten. The first eight chapters of the pupil text contain the core of the course. The material in these chapters is presented in a sequential pattern, and some teachers may wish to spend the whole of the time allotted to this module on this material, leaving ample time for demonstrations, theoretical work, practical work, discussion and, in particular, visits to local industries. An alternative strategy is to spend the first eight weeks on the material in Chapters 1 to 8, and then spend the remaining two or four weeks developing the core material along one of three optional lines.

Either 1   A consideration of more advanced sequential control circuits as detailed in Chapter 9.

Or 2   An introduction to air jet devices, systems and applications, and also logic circuits (Chapters 10 and 11). Although it requires additional equipment, this option is highly recommended. It introduces a range of sensing and logic control systems which complement and illuminate electronic sensing and logic systems, and are an excellent bridge to this branch of technology. Moreover, this option provides a good foundation for any advanced level technology course in which a study of automation is to be included. There is a considerable quantity of material in this option, and those with only two weeks available for it will need to prune it substantially, perhaps concentrating on air jet devices, systems and applications while omitting logic circuits.

Or 3   A mini project (Chapter 12). Activity 12 gives a selection of design briefs for mini projects. The groups of pupils should not be given a free choice of design brief. Apart from valuable time being lost while pupils pick and choose, the situation is avoided where two or more groups decide to tackle the same project. Another reason for the teacher allotting each group a design brief is that this is closer to the 'real life' situation where designers have to get on and deal with whatever their employer requires.

Chapter 12 and Activity 12 can also find a place in a course in which one of the other options is chosen. The material could be used for written homework assignments, several being set during the course. According to the extent of work expected, each assignment could be allowed a week or longer. If this approach is adopted, it is useful to set all the pupils the same problem to be tackled individually. When the work has been marked, the inevitable wide range of solutions to the same problem can be reviewed and evaluated. This helps pupils discover that there is no one right answer to a problem but rather that there are many possibilities, each with its own merits and demerits. A further benefit of this approach is that each pupil has to develop the ability to communicate his or her original thoughts and ideas through drawings, words, circuit diagrams, block diagrams, charts, symbols, graphs or some other appropriate means.

The practical work and the equipment in the Pneumatics Kit (see Section 3) is based on a class size of eighteen pupils who, it is assumed, will work in groups of three. It must be stressed: (a) that a class of eighteen is an absolute maximum to be avoided if at all possible; (b) that 'three is a crowd', i.e. a group of doubtful social worth in which a very uneven amount of 'hands on' experience with the equipment is highly likely; (c) that the quantity of equipment has been pared down to the absolute minimum consistent with a worthwhile course at the lowest possible initial cost. While experience in teaching the course is limited, and while there is total dependence on the basic kit, it is strongly recommended that only classes of twelve pupils working in groups of two be permitted. Even when experience is gained and facilities improve, maintenance of a working group size of two is highly desirable even if the size of the class increases.

The initial capital outlay required to set up a pneumatics course is high. A basic kit must be purchased, together with extra items which may be required for the selected option, and a compressed air supply system must be installed. This should be a full air line system with air piped to six or more check units conveniently placed round the technology room. However, this capital cost could be compared with the cost of a small and very modest lathe which can be used by only one pupil at a time! For a much smaller outlay, a pneumatics course can provide a number of pupils with a demanding and valuable educational experience year after year. In addition, the course has no consumables and the pneumatics equipment is extremely durable. It can be expected to give many years of trouble-free service. In cost-effective terms the course rates very highly indeed. This position is enhanced by the fact that the equipment stock can be improved with redundant but perfectly serviceable pneumatic components which local industries throw out for scrap, any other action on their part being uneconomical. At the earliest moment, contacts should be made with industry, either directly or through pupils' parents, so that this scrap equipment can be intercepted. Firms are usually only too pleased to find that a school can make good use of it.

When ex-industrial equipment is obtained, probably all that will be required is external cleaning and the fitting of the appropriate sized 'Plasticon' port adaptors. Occasionally, a surplus item will require replacement of an O-ring seal or a solenoid coil where the original is either burnt out or of a working voltage other than the 12 volts dc used by the kit components. Spares are usually easily obtained either from the original manufacturer or from a pneumatic equipment supplier. Surplus equipment may well differ in appearance from that illustrated in the text or in the kit. This does not matter and it causes pupils no problems, provided the component's pneumatic function is ascertained and understood. The equipment manufacturer's catalogue is a valuable identification aid and teachers are recommended to obtain catalogues from the major manufacturers. Appendix C lists various addresses.

Prior to the commencement of the course, thought must be given to the storage of the pneumatic equipment and the means by which it is best made available to pupils for practical work. It is a good plan to make available only what is required for the current Activity, as this avoids uninformed freelance experimentation. During practical work, pupils may simply lay components on the bench and pipe them up. This works quite satisfactorily even though the circuit's appearance is somewhat untidy. Some teachers may prefer to devise means of mounting components on a structure such as Hybridex. Economatics (see Appendix C) retail a Hybridex-based mounting system. This incorporates a busbar which makes multiple connections to the main air supply very easy, and avoids the use of a large number of T-connectors. For practical work involving mechanically signalled automatic and sequential circuits, the appropriate components must be rigidly mounted. A plywood or blockboard base to which components are fixed with brackets and screws is quite satisfactory. Details for such a system are given in Section 3.

In Section 4, air compressors and associated equipment are discussed. A compressor is a noisy machine and forward planning should include consideration of how best the noise level can be minimised. The ideal solution is to install the compressor in an adjacent, secure and ventilated outbuilding. Failing this, installation in a store room or a spacious built-in cupboard will be satisfactory. It is essential that such a situation be well ventilated, preferably directly by the air outside the building, as a compressor should breathe the coolest possible air.

The obvious benefits of establishing links with local industry are the possibility of class visits to see pneumatics in action, and the acquisition of surplus equipment. In addition, it is good to establish links with colleges of further education and polytechnics, as these may be able to loan additional pneumatic equipment to enhance and extend the practical work opportunities. Other resources for the course are slides, photographs, models and written articles on the social and industrial uses of pneumatics and fluid logic (fluidic) systems.

Before pupils are allowed to handle pneumatic equipment, it is of the utmost importance that they are made aware of the hazards of compressed air and the large forces which pneumatic cylinders can generate. Good standards of workshop/laboratory safety are essential at all times. Safety is mentioned in Section 5 of this handbook, while specific hazards and points of good procedure are set out inside the front cover of the Workbook. Teachers should check equipment at regular intervals to see that it is in good condition. It cannot be stressed too strongly that home-made air compressors and air receivers should not be manufactured, let alone used, in school.

Conceptual Diagram of the Pneumatics Module

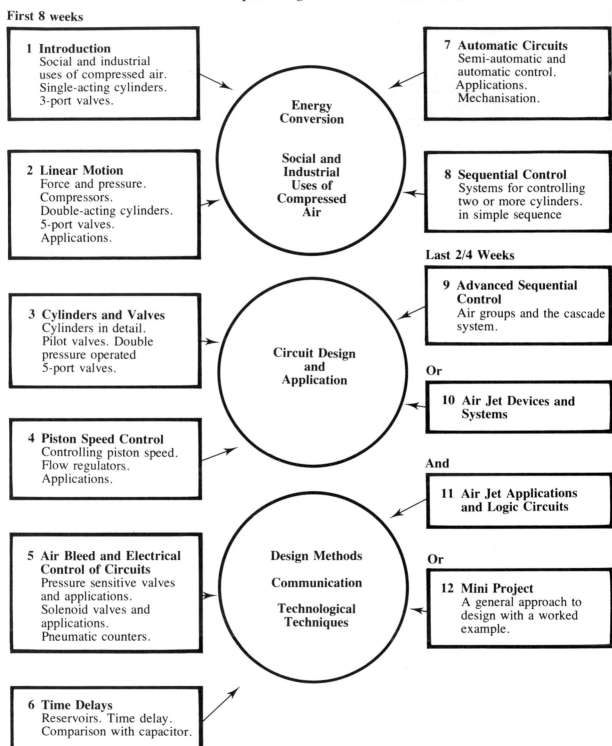

First 8 weeks

1 Introduction
Social and industrial uses of compressed air. Single-acting cylinders. 3-port valves.

2 Linear Motion
Force and pressure. Compressors. Double-acting cylinders. 5-port valves. Applications.

Energy Conversion

Social and Industrial Uses of Compressed Air

7 Automatic Circuits
Semi-automatic and automatic control. Applications. Mechanisation.

8 Sequential Control
Systems for controlling two or more cylinders. in simple sequence

Last 2/4 Weeks

3 Cylinders and Valves
Cylinders in detail. Pilot valves. Double pressure operated 5-port valves.

4 Piston Speed Control
Controlling piston speed. Flow regulators. Applications.

Circuit Design and Application

9 Advanced Sequential Control
Air groups and the cascade system.

Or

10 Air Jet Devices and Systems

And

11 Air Jet Applications and Logic Circuits

5 Air Bleed and Electrical Control of Circuits
Pressure sensitive valves and applications. Solenoid valves and applications. Pneumatic counters.

6 Time Delays
Reservoirs. Time delay. Comparison with capacitor.

Design Methods

Communication

Technological Techniques

Or

12 Mini Project
A general approach to design with a worked example.

Specific Aims

The module should enable the pupil to:
(a) apply a knowledge of pneumatics to solving design problems;
(b) be aware of the use of pneumatics in society and industry;
(c) understand the basic concepts and scientific principles of pneumatics;
(d) use pneumatic components in circuits, and build pneumatic circuits from circuit diagrams;
(e) give applications for pneumatic circuits and understand the function of individual components;
(f) apply basic communications techniques to problem solving situations;
(g) develop an awareness of safety factors related to pneumatics;
(h) apply a basic knowledge of materials and mechanisms to the study of pneumatics;
(i) develop a technological vocabulary and use it in relation to pneumatics;
(j) make simple calculations concerned with pneumatic design;
(k) compare pneumatic solutions to problems with alternative electronic, electrical or mechanical solutions, and evaluate their relative merits;
(l) develop practical skills in the use of pneumatic components and circuit construction;
(m) develop logical thinking by analysis of circuit functioning;
(n) appreciate compressed air as an energy store, its position in a long chain of energy conversions, and how this energy is used to do work.

Assumed Knowledge

The *Pneumatics* module can be taught to pupils with no prior knowledge of technology. Pneumatics is taught from first principles, and the assumed knowledge is what would be expected of pupils who have studied a three-year basic course in mathematics, science and technical studies.

Mathematics
(a) Basic arithmetic ability, including the multiplication and division of decimals and fractions.
(b) Use of indices and manipulation of large numbers, e.g. 10^5 means $10 \times 10 \times 10 \times 10 \times 10$ or 100 000.
(c) Use of simple equations and formulae, e.g. $F = p \times A$ where F is force, p is pressure and A is area.
(d) Changing the subject of a formula, e.g. if $F = p \times A$, then $p = F/A$.
(e) The ability to check that all the units in an equation agree, and to adjust them if required, e.g. changing metres to millimetres.
(f) Use of π (3.142) and the calculation of area of circles.

Science
(a) The concept of pressure – in particular atmospheric pressure.
(b) Knowledge of SI units of mass, length, time and force.
(c) Knowledge of simple electrical circuits involving lamps, switches and batteries is useful for logic work.
(d) For O-level pupils who take a theoretical look at pneumatic and fluidic devices,

knowledge of the gas laws is useful but not essential, e.g. Boyle's law, Charles' law and general gas equation:

$$\frac{P_1 V_1}{T_1} = \frac{P_2 V_2}{T_2}$$

Technical Studies

No practical knowledge is required for the early lessons. If pupils are given a mini project to complete the module, then basic practical skills and knowledge of processes are essential.

(a) Basic manipulative skills for timber, metal and plastics.

(b) Knowledge of elementary methods of joining, fabricating and fixing.

(c) Pupils should be able to use basic hand tools and machine tools such as the drilling machine, lathe and brazing hearth.

2 Detailed Notes for Teachers

Week No. and Content	Objectives To help pupils be able to:	Technological Interpretation and Applications
1 *Introduction to Pneumatics* Pneumatic systems Social and industrial uses of compressed air Pneumatic circuits and symbols The single-acting cylinder Applications of the single-acting cylinder Control of the single-acting cylinder – the 3-port valve The 3-port valve in detail Component details Controlling a single-acting cylinder from two positions	■ describe what is meant by 'pneumatics'; ■ draw a simple pneumatic system in block diagram form; ■ describe with sketches at least three uses of compressed air; ■ describe the construction of a single-acting cylinder; ■ draw the BSI/ISO symbol for a single-acting cylinder; ■ draw the symbol for a 3-port valve; ■ draw the control circuit for a single-acting cylinder; ■ use the numbering or lettering code on valve ports to pipe up simple control circuits; ■ describe the construction and operation of a shuttle valve; ■ draw the symbol for a shuttle valve; ☐ describe the construction of a 3-port valve; ■ draw a circuit with a single-acting cylinder controlled from two positions; ■ describe, with sketches, three applications of a single-acting cylinder.	Compression of air – stored energy. Ability to do work. Concept of a simple pneumatic system. Social and industrial applications of compressed air. Concept of linear motion and force from a single-acting cylinder. Use of graphic symbols for circuit diagrams. Use of port numbering codes. Concept of control of a single-acting cylinder from two positions. Consider the need for an exhaust air route. Personal experience of pneumatics – bicycle tyres and pumps, motor car tyres and garage compressors, spraying equipment, road drills, dentists' drills. Concept of personal safety – use of air lines.
2 *Linear Motion* Units of pressure Force from a pneumatic cylinder The compressor unit The double-acting cylinder Control of the double-acting cylinder 5-port valve control of a double-acting cylinder The 5-port valve in detail Types of 5-port valves and applications	■ state the SI units of pressure, force and area; ■ define the engineering unit of pressure – the bar; ■ state the relationship between force, pressure and area; ■ use the formula force = pressure × area in simple calculations; ■ draw a schematic labelled diagram of a compressor unit; ■ draw the symbol for a double-acting cylinder; ■ describe the control of a double-acting cylinder with two 3-port valves; ■ draw the symbol for a lever set/reset 5-port valve; ■ describe the operation of a 5-port valve to control a double-acting cylinder;	Concepts of pressure, area and force. Relationship between force, pressure and area. Use of SI units of force, pressure and area. Concept of compression of air. Strain in vessels under pressure. Compressibility of air. Filtration and lubrication of compressed air. Concept of double-acting cylinders – main air and exhaust air.

upil Activity	Teacher's Notes	Resources (Visual, Text, Hardware)	Lesson Requirements
pe up simple control of ngle-acting cylinder circuits ctivity 1, Assignments –3).	This is an introductory lesson, aimed at interesting pupils in pneumatics. Pupils' attention should be drawn to the uses of pneumatics in society and industry. Draw out examples and applications from the class. Use slides of applications of pneumatics in local industry.	Slides showing examples of social and industrial uses of compressed air.	Compressor and receiver.
pe up series and parallel mbinations of 3-port lves. Complete 'OR' and ND' truth tables for simple rcuits (Activity 1, ssignments 4 and 5).		Overhead projector transparencies (see Appendix B.)	Bicycle pump.
xamine a variety of 3-port lves.		Model of single-acting cylinder in clear perspex.	Single-acting cylinders, range of 3-port valves, shuttle valves, nylon tubes and fittings from Pneumatics Kit.
	A visit to a local factory might be possible.	Home-made model 3-port valve.	Squared paper (5 mm A4) is useful for pupils' circuit diagrams.
	Demonstrate the production of linear motion and force from compressed air – use of bicycle pump. Demonstrate piping up of single-acting cylinder. Have examples of different kinds of 3-port valves. Demonstrate piping of shuttle valve. Emphasise the safe use of air line equipment. Keep air lines away from eyes, ears, nose, mouth, and also cuts in skin.	Wallchart of 3-port valve – port numbering is useful. Martonair overhead projector transparencies of single-acting cylinder, shuttle valve and 3-port valve.	
lake simple calculations in tebook of force produced y a cylinder.	Explain how the force produced by a single-acting cylinder can be calculated from the formula: force = pressure × area. Revise the SI units of area. Explain the units used to measure force and pressure.	Slides of compressor units and air line equipment.	Access to a compressor unit.
xamine a compressor unit.		Overhead projector transparencies of a double-acting cylinder and 5-port valve.	Examples of filters, pressure regulators and lubricators.
xamine examples of uble-acting cylinders and port valves.		Home-made wallchart of numbering code for a 5-port valve.	Examples of double-acting cylinders and 5-port valves.
raw symbols in notebook of uble-acting cylinders and port valves.	Explain the function of the main parts of a compressor unit. Examine the compressor unit available, and/or slides of compressors and air line equipment. Appreciate the safe use of air line equipment.	Models of a double-acting cylinder and 5-port valve would be useful.	Squared paper (5 mm) is useful for circuit diagrams.
pe up circuits to control a uble-acting cylinder with o 3-port valves or a 5-port lve (Activity 2, ssignments 1–4).		Martonair overhead projector transparencies of 5-port valve and double-acting cylinder are excellent.	Double-acting cylinders, range of 3-port and 5-port valves, T-connectors, nylon tubes and fittings from Pneumatics Kit.
raw symbols in notebook of lve operating mechanisms d types of 5-port valves.			

Week No. and Content	Objectives To help pupils be able to:	Technological Interpretation and Applications
2 *Linear Motion* (continued)	■ draw a 5-port valve control circuit; □ describe the construction of a 5-port valve; ■ draw the symbols of three kinds of 5-port valve; ■ describe, with sketches, three applications of a 5-port valve.	Concept of control of double-acting cylinder with two valves or one valve. Use of lettering or numbering for 5-port valves. Concept of main air and exhaust air routes through a 5-port valve. Concept of valve operating mechanisms.
3 *Cylinders and Valves* Controlling two cylinders The single-acting cylinder and the double-acting cylinder The cushioned double-acting cylinder in detail The double pressure operated 5-port valve The double pressure operated 5-port valve in detail Control of a double-acting cylinder by one pilot valve Control of a double-acting cylinder by two pilot valves An application of remote pilot valve control	■ describe the construction of the single-acting cylinder and the double-acting cylinder; □ describe what is meant by a 'cushioned' cylinder stroke; ■ describe, with sketches, how control of two or more cylinders is achieved from one valve; ■ pipe up circuits controlling two cylinders from one valve; ■ describe applications of dual cylinder control; ■ draw the symbol for a double pressure operated 5-port valve; □ explain, with diagrams, how a double pressure operated 5-port valve works – by consideration of the sectioned valve; ■ pipe up circuits using a control valve and pilot valves; ■ describe an application of remote control of a cylinder; ■ draw a circuit with a double-acting cylinder controlled by pilot valves; ■ explain how the main air and exhaust air routes are determined; ■ decide which pilot valve was pressed last by inspection of the circuit.	Concept of spring return in cylinders and valves. Concept of 'cushioning' a cylinder. Concept of dual cylinder control from one valve. Use of T-connectors. Concept of air signals to operate a valve. Comparison of double pressure operated 5-port valve and bistable unit in electronics. Concept of a control valve and a pilot valve. Use of a double pressure operated 5-port valve as a control valve. Use of 5-port and 3-port valves as pilot valves. Graphical symbol for pilot lines. Concept of 'remote' control. The operation of a double pressure operated 5-port valve. Forces on a piston, using the equation: force = pressure × area.

Pupil Activity	Teacher's Notes	Resources (Visual, Text, Hardware)	Lesson Requirements
	Demonstrate piping up a double-acting cylinder with two 3-port valves. Demonstrate piping up a double-acting cylinder with a 5-port valve. Demonstrate the need for a four-way connector (two T-connectors linked by a short piece of tube).	Home-made model or animated wallchart of 5-port valve to show air routes.	
Examine industrial examples of cylinders. Draw symbol in notebook of double pressure operated -port valve. Examine double pressure operated 5-port valve. Pipe up circuits using the double pressure operated -port valve and various pilot valves. Pipe up dual cylinder control circuits. Pipe up AND' and 'OR' pilot valve control circuits. (Activity 3, Assignments 1–8.)	More advanced pupils could examine the working and construction of 5-port valves, 3-port valves and cylinders. Models or slides of sectioned components would help. Demonstrate how T-connectors can be used to enable two or more cylinders to be operated from one valve. Explain the numbering code for the ports of a double pressure operated 5-port valve. Explain the concept of a control valve and a pilot valve. Demonstrate how to pipe up a circuit with pilot valve control. Explain the reason for 'remote' control of a circuit – ask for examples from pupils. In the Workbook assignments, it is suggested that three groups tackle Assignments 5 and 6 while another three do Assignments 7 and 8. The groups can then change over assignments.	Any available slides of component sections. Overhead projector transparencies of double pressure operated 5-port valve. Home-made wallchart to show control and pilot valves would be useful.	Examples of cylinders obtained from local industry. Sectioned valves and cylinders useful. Double-acting and single-acting cylinders, range of 3-port and 5-port valves, shuttle valves, T-connectors, nylon tubes and fittings from Pneumatics Kit. Valve trip cams (can be made in school – see Section 3).

Week No. and Content	Objectives To help pupils be able to:	Technological Interpretation and Applications
4 *Piston Speed Control* Introduction The flow regulator in detail Controlling piston speed Applications of circuits with control of piston speed Cylinder force	■ explain, with the aid of sketches, how the speed of a piston can be controlled using a flow regulator; ■ recognise and draw the circuit diagram symbol for a flow regulator; ■ describe, with the aid of sketches, at least one application of the flow regulator with a single-acting cylinder, and two applications with a double-acting cylinder; ☐ use the equation force = $A(p_1 - p_2)$ for calculations on double-acting cylinders.	The concept of remote control of a double-acting cylinder using pilot valves (revision). The concept of piston speed and its control for instroke and outstroke of a cylinder. The placing of the flow regulator in the exhaust air route. Applications requiring piston speed control, such as packaging machines, vices, opening and closing windows. Apply the force equation force = pressure × area to a double-acting cylinder.
5 *Air Bleed and Electrical Control of Circuits* Pressure sensitive valves Air bleed circuits Applications for air bleed circuits Pressure sensing circuits Solenoid valves Using the solenoid valve The pneumatic counter	■ recognise and draw the circuit diagram symbol for a pressure sensitive, diaphragm operated valve; ■ explain, with the aid of sketches, what is meant by an air bleed circuit; ■ describe, with the aid of sketches, at least two applications of air bleed circuits; ■ pipe up a pressure sensing circuit from a circuit diagram; ■ describe one application of a pressure sensing circuit;	Concept of signal amplification by use of a diaphragm valve. Air bleed' concept – blocking the bleed and pressure build-up used to trip diaphragm valves. Applications of air bleed circuits, such as machine tool guard sensing, alarms and combination locks.

upil Activity	Teacher's Notes	Resources (Visual, Text, Hardware)	Lesson Requirements
/atch revision emonstration of pilot valve ontrol of a double-acting ylinder. lore able pupils can xamine sectioned 5-port alves. ipe up circuits using flow egulators and single-acting nd double-acting cylinders Activity 4, Assignments –7).	Demonstrate pilot valve control of a double-acting cylinder as revision. Consider the problem of trying to signal the 5-port valve from both signal ports. Allow more able pupils to examine sectioned 5-port valves (double pressure operated). Demonstrate the use of a flow regulator to control the piston speed of a double-acting cylinder and a single-acting cylinder. Slides of pupil projects which required piston speed control could be shown. With more able pupils, the advantages and disadvantages of exhaust line speed control over supply line speed control could be discussed In the Workbook assignments, it is suggested that three groups do Assignments 4 and 5 while another three do Assignments 6 and 7. The groups can then change over assignments. Examples of 'force' calculations can be set for homework.	Martonair overhead projector transparency of sectioned flow regulator. Home-made OHP transparency of flow regulator would be useful. Martonair OHP transparency of sectioned 5-port valve. Slide of sectioned 5-port valve. Model of a sectioned 5-port valve useful. Could be made in wood or plastic.	Sectioned 5-port valve would be useful – perhaps an old valve from local industry. Double-acting and single-acting cylinders, flow regulators, range of 3-port and 5-port valves, shuttle valves, T-connectors, nylon tubes and fittings from Pneumatics Kit.
xamine pressure sensitive -port valves. ipe up an air bleed circuit Activity 5, Assignment 1). ipe up a pressure sensing rcuit (Activity 5, ssignment 2). pe up circuits using olenoid valves for control of ouble-acting cylinders Activity 5, Assignments 3 d 4).	Demonstrate the action of a pressure sensitive valve by applying a high pressure air signal to the signal port. Demonstrate an air bleed circuit with a single-acting cylinder, then with a double-acting cylinder.	Overhead projector transparency of an air bleed circuit is useful. Slides of school projects involving air bleed circuits. Martonair overhead projector transparency of the solenoid valve is useful. Home-made OHP transparency could be used.	Double-acting cylinders, flow regulators, range of 3-port and 5-port valves, shuttle valves, microswitches, T-connectors, nylon tubes and fittings from Pneumatics Kit. 12 V dc power supply. Pneumatic counter.

Week No. and Content	Objectives To help pupils be able to:	Technological Interpretation and Applications
5 *Air Bleed and Electrical Control of Circuits* (continued)	■ recognise and draw the circuit diagram symbol for a solenoid valve; ■ pipe up a pilot valve control circuit using a solenoid valve; ■ recognise and draw the circuit diagram symbol for a pneumatic counter; ■ describe, with the aid of a sketch, one application of a pneumatic counter.	Sensing a falling exhaust pressure – its use to detect piston position. Applications of pressure sensing circuits. Advantages of using a solenoid valve. Applications of solenoid valves for electrical control of pneumatic circuits. Applications of the pneumatic counter. Comparison of pneumatic counter with electromagnetic counter and mechanical counter.
6 *Time Delays* The reservoir Time delay in pneumatic circuits Time delay circuit applications A more complex time delay circuit Reservoir volume Comparison of systems Using a reservoir with a single-acting cylinder	■ recognise and draw the circuit diagram symbol for a reservoir; ■ describe how a time delay is achieved pneumatically; ■ draw and explain the action of a basic time delay circuit; ■ describe, with the aid of a sketch, an application of a time delay circuit; ■ draw and explain the action of a more complex time delay circuit which uses a feedback signal from a T-connector in the main air supply to the cylinder; ■ recognise that pneumatic time delay is associated with reservoir volume and rate of filling; □ name an electronic component equivalent to the pneumatic reservoir; ■ describe, with the aid of a sketch, the time delay control of a single-acting cylinder; ■ draw and recognise the circuit diagram symbol for a lever set/reset 3-port valve.	The concept of time delay with respect to pneumatics. The analogy of water tanks used to explain air reservoirs. Applications of time delay circuits. Feedback of air signals through a reservoir and flow regulator. Reciprocating cylinder – piston motion caused by double time delay. Concept of reservoir volume proportional to time delay. Comparison of electronic and pneumatic systems for creating time delay.

upil Activity	Teacher's Notes	Resources (Visual, Text, Hardware)	Lesson Requirements
evise 'AND-OR' circuits Activity 5, Assignments 5 nd 6).	Solenoid valves are often given away by local industry. Care should be taken to use only low voltage (12 or 24 V dc) solenoid valves with school pupils. Initiate a group discussion of the meaning of 'solenoid', and its uses in other branches of technology. In the Workbook assignments, it is suggested that two groups tackle Assignments 1 and 2, while another two tackle Assignments 3 and 4, and another two Assignments 5 and 6. The groups then change assignments in rotation. Demonstrate the action of a pneumatic counter.	Examples of electro-magnetic counters and mechanical counters might be useful.	
ipe up time delay circuits ivolving single-acting and ouble-acting cylinders Activity 6, Assignments 1 nd 2). ipe up time delay return rcuits and air bleed time elay return circuits (Activity , Assignments 3 and 4).	Demonstrate the principle of time delay by filling a tank with water, the water flow being controlled by a valve or flow regulator. Demonstrate two basic time delay circuits. Useful to note that a long length of nylon pipe can be used as a reservoir. One end of a cylinder can also be used as a reservoir. Demonstrate a complex time delay circuit and a double time delay circuit. Two lengths of nylon tube can be used for double time delay circuits. More able pupils might consider the mathematics of calculating reservoir volumes. They could also discuss the electronic components (capacitors and resistors) used to produce time delay.	Models of water tanks are useful to demonstrate how time delay depends on reservoir size. Overhead projector transparencies of reservoir and time delay circuits. Slides of pupil projects using reservoirs.	Double-acting and single-acting cylinders, flow regulators, reservoirs, range of 3-port and 5-port valves, T-connectors, nylon tubes and fittings from Pneumatics Kit. Stopwatch or wristwatch with seconds hand.

Week No. and Content	Objectives To help pupils be able to:	Technological Interpretation and Applications
7 *Automatic Circuits* Semi-automatic control Automatic control Comparison of systems Alternative automatic circuits Automatic circuit applications Mechanisation	■ describe, with the aid of sketches, the action of a pilot valve control circuit; ■ describe, with the aid of sketches, how pilot valves can be used to produce semi-automatic control of a cylinder; ■ describe what is meant by reciprocating piston motion; □ compare pneumatic, electronic and other control systems, and note similarity of operation; ■ describe, with the aid of circuit diagrams, at least two methods of achieving automatic control of a double-acting cyinder; ■ describe, with a circuit diagram, how to achieve on/off control in an automatic cycle control circuit; ■ describe, with the aid of sketches, at least two applications of automatic control circuits; ■ describe, with the aid of sketches, the meaning of 'mechanisation'.	Concept of 'pilot valve' control of cylinders. Concept of semi-automatic control of cylinders. Cylinder motion – distinguish between reciprocati• and oscillation. Concept of automatic control of a double-acting cylinder – application of roller-trip valves, pressure sensitive valves, solenoid valves. Applications of automatic control circuits. Concept of 'mechanisation' and the steps involved between manual labour and pneumatic mechanisation.
8 *Sequential Control* The need for sequential control Achieving sequential control Continuous cycle sequential control Another example of sequential control Time delay sequential control Sequential control of three cylinders	■ explain the meaning of sequential control by describing a sequence of piston movements; ■ from a circuit diagram, pipe up a simple sequential control circuit, e.g. $A+$, $B+$, $A-$, $B-$ or $A+$, $B-$, $A-$, $B+$; ■ explain, with the aid of a circuit diagram, the operation of a sequential control circuit such as $A+$, $B+$, $A-$, $B-$ or $A+$, $B-$, $A-$, $B+$; □ explain, with the aid of a circuit diagram, the operation of a time delay sequential control circuit; □ from a circuit diagram, pipe up a simple sequential control circuit that uses reservoirs to provide time delay.	Concept of sequential control of cylinder piston movements. Application of sequential control systems, such as a plastics press, that use two cylinders. Application of a 'circular diagram' to assist the understanding of a continuous cycle sequential control circuit. Application of the concept of time delay to sequence the operation of cylinders.

Pupil Activity	Teacher's Notes	Resources (Visual, Text, Hardware)	Lesson Requirements
Pipe up a variety of automatic control circuits using roller-trip valves, pressure sensitive valves, reservoirs and solenoid valves (Activity 7, Assignments 1–5).	Demonstrate a semi-automatic control circuit using roller-trip and plunger operated pilot valves. Demonstrate several automatic control circuits using roller-trip valves, reservoirs, pressure sensitive valves and solenoids. For the Workbook assignments, it is suggested that the groups arc organised as follows (six groups of three pupils): first two groups do Assignment 1, second two groups Assignment 2, third group Assignment 4, fourth group Assignment 5. The groups should then change assignments in rotation. Assignment 3 could be tackled by a combination of two groups which have completed both Assignments 1 and 2, and are awaiting equipment for Assignment 4 or 5.	Overhead projector transparencies of semi-automatic and automatic control circuits. Slides of pupil projects involving automatic control circuits. Slides of automation systems in local industry would be useful.	Double-acting cylinders, flow regulators, reservoirs, range of 3-port and 5-port valves, shuttle valves, microswitches, nylon tubes and fittings from Pneumatics Kit. 12 V dc power supply.
Pipe up simple sequential control circuits, e.g. $A+$, $B+$, $A-$, $B-$ or $A+$, $B-$, $A-$, $B+$ (Activity 8, Assignments 1 and 2). Pipe up sequential control circuits using reservoirs to produce time delay (Activity 8, Assignment 3). Written exercise – possibly for homework (Activity 8, Assignment 4).	This lesson requires either additional equipment (which may often be loaned by a local polytechnic or college of further education) or a reduction in the number of working groups from six to three, each group tackling one of the first three assignments in turn. Assignment 4 is a written exercise suitable for O-level pupils, and may be done either in class or as homework. Demonstrate the piping up of simple sequential control circuits.	Useful Martonair booklet *The Martonair Cascade System of Circuit Analysis* – mainly suitable for teacher use. *Circuit Design* booklet from Maxam is useful. Overhead projector transparencies from Appendix B are very useful. Slides might be useful to describe the need for sequential operation of cylinders.	Double-acting cylinders, flow regulators, reservoirs, range of 3-port and 5-port valves, T-connectors, nylon tubes and fittings from Pneumatics Kit. Some pre-printed A4 sheets giving cylinder and valve outlines should be available for completion by pupils – could be made from OHP master No. 16 in Appendix B.

Week No. and Content	Objectives To help pupils be able to:	Technological Interpretation and Applications
8 *Sequential Control* (continued)		
9/ 10 *Advanced Sequential Control* (optional – will probably require two or three weeks) An application of sequential control An inoperable circuit The cascade system Another example of the cascade system Sequential control of three cylinders	☐ write down the cylinder movement sequence for a known example such as a pneumatic machine vice and power drill; ☐ explain the need for a cascade system by the use of an inoperable circuit; ☐ from a circuit diagram, pipe up a complex sequential control circuit, e.g. $A+, B+, B-, A-;$ $A+, A-, B+, B-;$ $A+, B+, C+, A-, C-, B-;$ $A+, B+, B-, C+, C-, A-.$	Application of sequential control – machine vice and power drill operation. The concept of an inoperable circuit. The application of a cascade system to control air groups. Use of circular diagrams to describe cylinder sequences. The use of a busbar to supply air groups.
9/ 10 *Air Jet Devices and Systems* (optional – will probably require two weeks, and should be used in conjunction with *Air Jet Applications and Logic Circuits*) Sensing systems Low pressure supply of oil-free air	■ describe how pressure sensing is used instead of mechanical trip valves to detect the position of a piston; ■ draw a pressure sensing circuit; ■ explain what is meant by a 'sensor' in a control circuit; ■ define the unit of measurement of low pressure (the millibar – mbar);	Concept of 'pressure sensing' of fall in exhaust air pressure. Use of low pressure air devices. Concept of control circuits – 'control' of pneumatics or electrics; Low pressure measurement and supply.

Pupil Activity	Teacher's Notes	Resources (Visual, Text, Hardware)	Lesson Requirements
	Demonstrate how reservoirs can be used to give a time delay sequential control. Worthwhile arranging visits to local factories to observe automation systems in operation.		
Pipe up complex sequential control circuits, e.g. A+, B+, B−, A−; A+, A−, B+, B−; A+, B+, B−, C+, C−, A − (Activity 9, Assignments 1−4). Written exercise – possibly for homework (Activity 9, Assignment 5).	Consider the operation of a pneumatic machine vice and power drill. Demonstrate the use of manifolds/busbars for air group selection. Demonstrate examples of complex sequential control circuits that require the cascade system. This lesson requires additional equipment – investigate the possibility of borrowing sequential circuit boards from a local polytechnic or college of further education. If the number of working groups is reduced to three, each group can tackle the first three assignments in rotation. Assignment 4 is a complex circuit and is optional. Assignment 5 is a written exercise which can be done in class or as homework. Local factory visits worthwhile.	Martonair booklet *The Martonair Cascade System of Circuit Analysis* is useful for teachers. Overhead projector transparencies are useful as they save drawing very complex diagrams on the blackboard. Slides of pupil projects that use sequential control.	Double-acting cylinders, range of 3-port and 5-port valves, T-connectors, nylon tubes and fittings from Pneumatics Kit. Sequential control boards. Pre-printed A4 sheets giving cylinder and valve outlines for pupils to complete – Fig. 9.1 in the Workbook could be used as a master.
Pipe up a pressure sensing circuit (Activity 10, Assignment 1). Draw symbols for low pressure jet detection equipment in notebook. Pipe up a jet occlusion circuit (Activity 10, Assignment 2).	This lesson and the next can only be attempted if an extra kit of air jet devices and fluidic equipment is available in addition to the basic Pneumatics Kit. (See Section 3 for details.)	*Detection and Sensing with Air Jets* by J. E. Graham from Martonair is a very useful booklet. Home-made overhead projector transparencies would be useful.	Unlubricated air supply is essential for fluidic and jet detection circuits. It is desirable that the unlubricated supply has check units different from those on the lubricated supply. An alternative is a T-junction in the air line before the lubricator,

Week No. and Content	Objectives To help pupils be able to:	Technological Interpretation and Applications
9/ 10 *Air Jet Devices and Systems* (continued) Air bleed jet occlusion systems Contactless sensing systems The proximity sensor Fluid flow Interruptible jet systems Dusty atmospheres Long distance gap sensor Connecting low pressure devices	■ draw the symbol for a pressure regulator and a unidirectional flow regulator; ■ explain what is meant by a jet detection system; ■ draw a jet occlusion circuit using an amplifier valve or a diaphragm valve; ■ draw the symbol for an amplifier valve; ■ draw the symbol for a touch sensor; ■ describe, with sketches, an application of a touch sensor; ■ describe what is meant by laminar flow; ■ draw an interruptible jet system and describe an application; ■ draw the symbol for an emitter and collector; ■ draw the symbol for a gap sensor and describe an application; ■ draw the symbol for a proximity sensor and describe an application; ■ describe what is meant by 'turbulence'; ■ describe, with sketches, the principle of a turbulence amplifier; ■ draw the symbol for a long distance gap sensor and describe, with sketches, its application; ■ draw a pressurised jet receiver circuit and state the environments in which it is used.	Use of low pressure fittings. Concept of jet occlusion. Application of jet occlusion – methods of occluding a jet. Concept of amplification of a low pressure signal. Use of touch sensors. Application of touch sensors. Concept of laminar flow and its application for interruptible jets. Use of emitters and collectors. Applications of a gap sensor. Concept of proximity sensing. Application of proximity sensors. Use of a pneumatic counter. Concept of the turbulence amplifier and its application. Concept of turbulence. Use of a long distance gap sensor. Use of sensors in dusty environments.
11/ 12 *Air Jet Applications and Logic Circuits* (optional – will probably require two weeks, and should be used in conjunction with *Air Jet Devices and Systems*) Air jet system applications Logic Pneumatic switching logic The bistable unit (FLIP-FLOP)	■ describe, with sketches, at least three applications for jet detection systems; □ explain the use of logic in control system design; □ use the words 'AND', 'OR' and 'NOT' in logic statements; □ draw the symbols used to indicate 'AND', 'OR' and 'NOT'; □ draw a pneumatic 'AND' circuit and an 'OR' circuit; □ complete a truth table for 'OR' and 'AND' circuits (2-input and 3-input circuits); □ describe the use of a double pressure operated 5-port valve as a bistable device;	Applications of jet detection systems: counting small objects and rotations; sensing presence or absence of components. Safety circuits using jet detection equipment. The concept of 'AND', 'OR' and 'NOT' in logic statements. Graphical representation with truth tables. Use of 3-port valves in series and parallel. Use of shuttle valves. Concept of a bistable device.

Pupil Activity	Teacher's Notes	Resources (Visual, Text, Hardware)	Lesson Requirements
Pipe up a touch sensor circuit (Activity 10, Assignment 3). Pipe up an interruptible jet system and use an emitter and collector (Activity 10, Assignment 4). Pipe up a gap sensor circuit (Activity 10, Assignment 5). Pipe up a proximity sensor circuit (Activity 10, Assignment 6).	Discuss the meaning and use of fluidics – mention could be made of the historical development. Explain the need for supply of unlubricated air. Demonstrate how low pressure air supply is achieved with a pressure regulator, gauge and unidirectional flow regulator. Explain how low pressure fittings are used. Demonstrate jet occlusion and touch sensor circuits. Demonstrate the principle of laminar flow, perhaps with a model. Demonstrate a gap sensor circuit and a proximity sensor circuit. Explain the concept of turbulence and how a turbulence amplifier works. Demonstrate the long distance gap sensor circuit. Demonstrate its use for air stream detection. Discuss applications of jet detection circuits. Each group should tackle a different assignment in turn.	A model made of plastic or glass tube and a chemistry laboratory rubber tube would be useful to demonstrate laminar flow. Teacher/technician will have to make up some occlusion jets and a collector.	connected to its low pressure regulator. Air Jet Devices and Logic Circuits Option Kit. Double-acting and single-acting cylinders, flow regulators, range of 3-port and 5-port valves, T-connectors, nylon tubes and fittings from main Pneumatics Kit. Jet occlusion plates and collectors (these can be made in school – see Section 3 for details) Pneumatic counter.
Draw symbols in notebook for a long distance gap sensor. Pipe up a long distance gap sensor circuit (Activity 11, Assignment 1). Pipe up a pressurised receiver jet circuit (Activity 11, Assignment 2). Pipe up pneumatic 'AND', 'OR' and 'NOT' circuits (Activity 11, Assignments 3–6).	This is a continuation of the previous lesson and provides an opportunity to introduce some logic work. The Boolean algebra element of the course could be developed in mathematics lessons. The application of Boolean algebra operations could be extremely useful, although they have not been fully developed in this course.	*Detection and Sensing with Air Jets* booklet by J. E. Graham from Martonair. *Introduction to Digital Fluidics, A Guide to Practical Fluidic Circuits* and *Norgren Fluidics Product Review* all available from IMI Norgren Ltd. Project Technology Handbook No. 4 *Introducing Fluidics*.	Unlubricated air supply. Air Jet Devices and Logic Circuits Option Kit. Single-acting and double-acting cylinders, flow regulators, 3-port and 5-port valves, shuttle valves, T-connectors, nylon tubes and fittings from main Pneumatics Kit. Collectors (made in school).

Week No. and Content	Objectives To help pupils be able to:	Technological Interpretation and Applications
11/ 12 *Air Jet Applications and Logic Circuits* (continued) An example of pneumatic logic Fluid logic (fluidic) devices	☐ describe, with sketches, an application of a logic circuit; ☐ explain the meaning of 'fluid logic'; ☐ explain the Coanda effect and its applications.	Applications of logic circuits. Coanda effect and its application in fluid logic (fluidic) devices.
9/ 12 Mini projects (optional – will require between two and four weeks) Introduction Projects A mini project timetable An example of problem solving – a fabric tester	■ write a report on a mini project to include the following steps – brief and/or specification, analysis of problem and investigation, alternative solutions, selecting a solution, realisation, testing and evaluation; ■ design a pneumatic circuit to solve a problem; ■ pipe up a prototype circuit; ■ test and evaluate the circuit.	Concept of 'project work' for pupils. Examination of mini project steps. Stating the need. Specifying the constraints. Problem analysis. Data collection, time plans. Selection of alternative solutions, optimisation. Graphical and visual communication of solutions – sketching, drawing graphs, circuits, charts, block diagrams, etc. Design of prototype. Manufacture of prototype. Realisation of a solution. Testing prototype. Recording test results. Evaluation of prototype. Modifications and future improvements. Conclusions.

Pupil Activity	Teacher's Notes	Resources (Visual, Text, Hardware)	Lesson Requirements
	Teacher awareness of electronic logic devices, e.g. TTL and CMOS integrated circuits, is desirable (see 'School Technology' magazine issues 46 and 47 of 1978 for a brief introduction). Each group can tackle a different assignment in turn.	Home-made overhead projector transparencies would be useful.	
Mini project selected from Activity 12.	The mini project is one of the options for the last two to four weeks of the course. Pupils can work in groups of two or three according to the quantity of pneumatic/fluidic equipment available. The pupils can choose from the list given in Activity 12 or the teacher may wish to allocate mini projects. This may be the most appropriate strategy as the assignment mini projects vary in complexity. Additional mini project ideas could be added to Activity 12 by the teacher. Emphasis can be placed on the designing of the circuit, the building of the prototype and the testing of the system, rather than on the writing of a report. In selecting the mini project, the availability of suitable equipment should be borne in mind.	Mini project report form drawn up by the teacher would be useful. Overhead projector transparency could be made up by the teacher to emphasise the important stages of the project. Examples of pupil project reports from previous years.	Pneumatics Kit. Possibly Air Jet Devices and Logic Circuits Option Kit. Construction kit structural members, e.g. Meccano, Hybridex, Dexion, Handy Angle, etc. Offcuts of timber, metal, plastic, etc.

3 List of Equipment

A complete kit comprising all the items below (sufficient for eighteen pupils working in groups of three) is available from Economatics Ltd, 4 Orgreave Crescent, Dore House Industrial Estate, Handsworth, Sheffield S13 9NQ. Order as 'Econ. 239 Modular Pneumatics Kit'.

Quantity	Description	Part No.	Manufacturer/Supplier
2	Minor double-acting cylinder, 1¼'' bore, 50 mm stroke	M/549/50	Martonair
2	Minor double-acting cylinder, 1¼'' bore, 150 mm stroke	M/549/150	
2	Minor double-acting cylinder, 1¼'' bore, 300 mm stroke	M/549/300	
6	Midget single-acting cylinder, ¾'' bore, 25 mm stroke	M/775/25	
2	Reservoir	S/810/13	
2	Reservoir	S/810/25	
8	Unidirectional flow regulator	S/836	
6	5-port valve, double pressure operated	43004PP	Schrader Bellows
3	5-port valve, lever set/reset	43004LS	
2	3-port valve, push-button operated	43603B	
8	3-port valve, roller-trip operated	43603R	
2	3-port valve, diaphragm operated spool valve	43003DS	
2	3-port valve, solenoid operated, 12 volt dc	154TA	
4	3-port valve, plunger operated	43603C	
10	Shuttle valve ⅛'' BSP	43005	
1	Air-operated counter	997-63-00-2	Crouzet
180	Plasticon port adaptor, ⅛'' BSP to 5 mm o.d. nylon tube	3030611	GKN Screws and Fasteners
10	Plasticon port adaptor, ¼'' BSP to 5 mm o.d. nylon tube	3031211	
30	Plasticon T-connector, joins three 5 mm o.d. nylon tubes	4030311	
5	Plasticon connector, joins two 5 mm o.d. nylon tubes	4030211	
15 m	5 mm o.d. nylon tube, red	NM5MM	Economatics
15 m	5 mm o.d. nylon tube, blue	NM5MM	
15 m	5 mm o.d. nylon tube, yellow	NM5MM	
1	Barbed connector (for counter)	3122-04-05	
1 reel	PTFE Tape		
2	Microswitch, roller operated	337–863	RS Components

In addition to the above kit, the following are required. (Note that Economatics can also supply all but the last of these. Enquire for details.)

Quantity	Description
6	Valve trip cams (can be made in school – see Fig. 3.5 for details)
6 + 6	Cylinder mounting brackets for fastening cylinders to baseboards when required (can be made in school – see Fig. 3.6 for details)
1	Compressed air supply system comprising a compressor, receiver, filter, regulator with gauge, lubricator, check units with plug-in adaptors having a ⅛″ BSP female thread, etc. See Section 4 for full details. Bear in mind the air supply requirements of the 'Air Jet Devices and Logic Circuits' option in the course when deciding on a system.
1	Nylon tube cutter
2	Power supply units, 12 volts, 1 amp, for solenoid valves

Prior to the first run of the course, preparatory work must be done on the compressed air supply system and on the equipment supplied in the kit. The commissioning of equipment is time consuming and should not be rushed. Plenty of time should also be allowed for full personal familiarisation with the course material and the equipment. Participation in an in-service training course is strongly advised.

Each cylinder, small reservoir, shuttle valve and flow regulator must have a Plasticon ⅛″ BSP to 5 mm o.d. nylon tube port adaptor securely screwed into each port. The two large reservoirs require Plasticon ¼″ BSP to 5 mm o.d. nylon tube port adaptors in their ports.

The 5-port valves require Plasticon ⅛″ BSP to 5 mm o.d. nylon tube port adaptors in all their ports except the exhaust ports. These two ports are either numbered 3 and 5, or lettered C and E, or possibly labelled 'EXH'. Recently manufactured valves will be numbered.

The 3-port valves, with the exception of the diaphragm operated valves, require Plasticon ⅛″ BSP to 5 mm o.d. nylon tube port adaptors in all ports except the exhaust port. This port is either numbered 3, or lettered C, or labelled 'EXH'. Recently manufactured valves will be numbered. The diaphragm operated 3-port valves must have a Plasticon ⅛″ BSP to 5 mm o.d. nylon tube port adaptor in all ports except that used to operate the valve by a vacuum signal.

The kit contains a slight excess of Plasticon ⅛″ BSP and ¼″ BSP to 5 mm o.d. nylon tube port adaptors. This is to allow additional new or secondhand equipment to be commissioned without delay.

Note that some valves do not have a tapped exhaust port, only a shrouded vent. The two 3-port solenoid operated valves are a case in point. These two valves must be wired up as follows.

1 Loosen the terminal cover screw.
2 Pull off the terminal cover.
3 Remove the hexagon ended plastic cable collet retainer from the terminal cover.
4 Remove the exposed collet from the terminal cover.
5 Remove a rubber washer and then a steel washer from the terminal cover.
6 Inside the terminal cover, unscrew the plastic central terminal block retaining screw.
7 Remove the terminal block from the cover.
8 Connect wires to terminals 1 and 2. The earth connection is not required in this application. Use wire of a diameter large enough to be gripped securely by the collet. One metre of wire should suffice.
9 Reassemble in reverse dismantling order. Note that the terminal block was in the

cover with the earth terminal furthest from the collet. If the more desirable horizontal, rather than downwards, cable exit from the collet is required, the terminal block may be repositioned accordingly. Note that the steel washer is put in the terminal cover before the rubber washer and the collet.

10   Halfway along the wire from each solenoid valve, connect a microswitch. Use the 'normally open' switch poles. The switch can be fixed to a small piece of plywood or plastic sheet with the wire looped in and out of two pairs of holes so that the connections to the switch are not strained in use (see Fig. 3.1).

Fig. 3.1   Connecting microswitch to valve

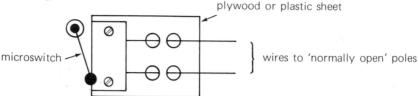

11   Fix terminals to the end of the wire for easy connection to the available power supply. A power supply of 12 volt, 1 amp, will operate the valves satisfactorily.

Nylon tube must be cut into suitable lengths. Lengths of 300 mm, 600 mm and 900 mm in each of the three colours are suggested. A one metre length of tube for each check unit's plug-in adaptor will be required.

Nylon tube can be cut with a craft knife or sharp side cutters. However, this tends to distort the end of the tube and so the use of the inexpensive tube cutter marketed by Economatics is recommended. Each end of each tube must be fitted with a Plasticon Slimline tubing nut assembly. Full details are given in Fig. 3.2

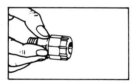  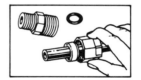 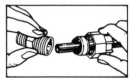

Fig. 3.2   (a) Screw cap assembly on to body for half of the thread length
            (b) Push home tube until it bottoms firmly
            (c) Unscrew cap and tube from body. Take rubber O-ring from pack and place on tube
            (d) Replace tube into body and screw up cap finger-tight

The two functions of sealing and retaining are performed by separate components. Compressed against the outside wall of the tube, the rubber O-ring forms an extremely effective seal. A stainless steel grab washer grips the tube and retains it within the fitting (Fig. 3.3). No preparation of the tube is needed other than a clean cut end.

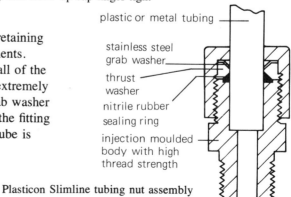

Fig. 3.3   Plasticon Slimline tubing nut assembly

The rubber O-rings on the tube ends are fairly secure. However, they should be checked from time to time and replacements installed as necessary. The stainless steel grab washer is normally within the nut and unexposed. However, its outer edge has a sharp burr which needs to be avoided should it become exposed.

The main components of Plasticon are injection moulded in nylon 66, a material which gives unlimited durability in normal indoor conditions. There are no toxic effects with the majority of liquid foodstuffs and beverages, and nylon 66 is resistant to common organic solvents and oils. The standard version of the sealing ring is made of nitrile rubber and is resistant to aliphatic hydrocarbons, aromatic hydrocarbons, oxygenated solvents, dilute acids, alkalis, salts, petroleum, oils, greases and synthetic lubricants. Working temperatures are normally −20°C to 80°C for prolonged exposure, but can be higher under certain conditions.

By virtue of its design, Plasticon has a high vibration resistance and a high pull-out strength. These qualities together with its great durability offer reliable and permanent installations. As well as pneumatic and low pressure hydraulic equipment, Plasticon is eminently suitable for systems handling a variety of gases, fuels, lubricants, chemicals and liquid foods.

Properties of Plasticon Fittings

PHYSICAL

Water absorption	24 h at 23°C	=	1·3%
	Saturation	=	8·5%

MECHANICAL

Elongation at break	40–80%
Flexural modulus	2850 Mn/m²
Shear strength	66 Mn/m²
Tensile strength	86 Mn/m²

THERMAL

Melting point	264°C

CHEMICAL		EFFECT
Acetone	100%	A
Ammonia	10%	A
Ammonia, gaseous	–	B/C
Benzene	100%	A
Bromine	100%	D
Bromine water	30%	D
Carbon tetrachloride	100%	A
Chlorine	10%	D
Chlorine water	–	D
Detergents	–	A
Diesel oil	–	A
Edible fats and oils	–	A
Formaldehyde	40%	A
Fruit juices	–	A
Mineral oils	–	A
Oils of vegetables	–	A
Paraffin	–	A
Petrol	–	A
Soap solution	–	A
Sodium chloride	10–90%	A
Sodium hydroxide	10%	A
	50%	B/C
Sulphuric acid	2%	C
above	5%	D
Transformer oil	–	A
Trichlorethylene	–	A/B
Vinegar	–	B/C
Water, cold	–	A
Water, hot	–	B

A – no attack; B – little or no attack, reduction of mechanical properties at 20°C; C – some attack, limited life; D – material decomposes at 20°C in short time.

Nylon tube is very forgiving, but if curved through a very small radius it will kink and cause a circuit to fail to operate. The kink is a permanent defect and should be cut out and the Slimline tubing nut refitted.

The kit includes Plasticon T-connectors which allow a tube to branch two ways. Frequently a tube needs to branch three ways. As no Plasticon fitting is available for this purpose, teachers may find it convenient to permanently link, by a very short piece of tube, twelve of the T-connectors to form six four-way connectors.

Various manufacturers produce check units with plug-in adaptors. Ensure that, whichever make is purchased, the plug-in adaptor has a ⅛″ BSP female thread. Into this must be screwed a Plasticon ⅛″ BSP to 5 mm o.d. nylon tube port adaptor. Sufficient are included in the kit for this purpose. Figure 3.4 shows the Schrader check unit and plug-in adaptor.

Fig. 3.4　The Schrader check unit and plug-in adaptor

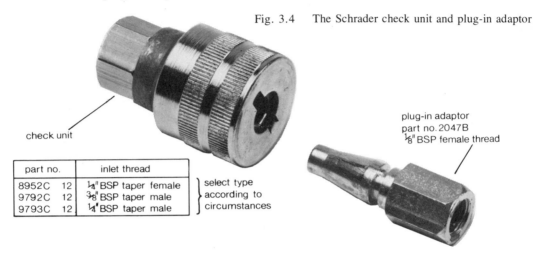

check unit

plug-in adaptor
part no. 2047B
⅛″ BSP female thread

part no.		inlet thread
8952C	12	¼″ BSP taper female
9792C	12	⅜″ BSP taper male
9793C	12	¼″ BSP taper male

} select type
} according to
} circumstances

It is a good idea to protect the piston rod threads of the six single-acting cylinders in the kit with small aluminium caps. The caps should be internally threaded M8 × 1.25 to a depth of 12 mm.

Each double-acting cylinder should have a valve trip cam (see Fig. 3.5 for details) fitted to the end of its piston rod. Apart from protecting the piston rod thread, valve trip cams are required when automatic and semi-automatic circuits are piped up. In many of these circuits, valves are operated by direct physical contact of the piston rod with the valve mechanism.

Fig. 3.5　Valve trip cam

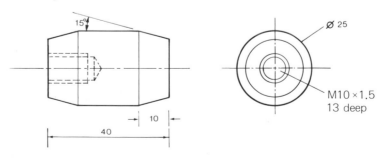

15°

Ø 25

M10×1.5
13 deep

10

40

34

The Activities associated with Chapters 7, 8 and 9 of the text require that double-acting cylinders and roller-trip and plunger operated 3-port valves are fastened on to baseboards. The valves are positioned so that the trip cam on the end of a piston rod will operate a valve at either end of its stroke. Teachers should carefully study the requirements of these Activities well in advance. The six double-acting cylinders can be fastened to six blockboard or plywood bases with the mounting brackets detailed in Fig. 3.6. The cylinder nose bracket is screwed to the baseboard. The rear bracket is bolted to the cylinder tie rods with M6 nuts and washers. The nose of the cylinder is passed through the 16 mm diameter hole in its bracket. The rear bracket is then screwed down.

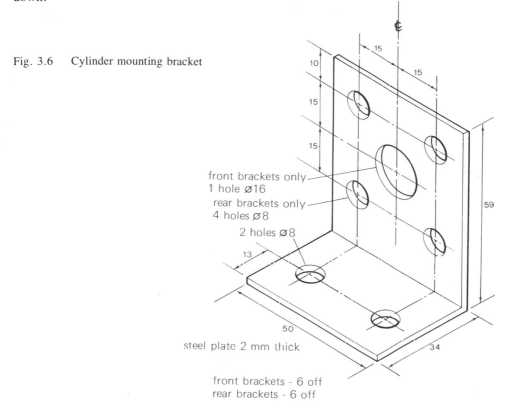

Fig. 3.6   Cylinder mounting bracket

front brackets only
1 hole ⌀16
rear brackets only
4 holes ⌀8
2 holes ⌀8

steel plate 2 mm thick

front brackets - 6 off
rear brackets - 6 off

The valves are mounted horizontally and secured to the baseboard by screws passed through the holes in their bodies. Packing should be placed under a valve body so that the height of its horizontal centre line above the board is the same as that of the cylinder. When securing a valve, check that the trip cam on the cylinder operates the valve properly but without causing the valve mechanism to 'bottom' (Fig. 3.7). Adjustment is facilitated by securing a valve with one screw, rotating the valve about that screw until operation is correct and then inserting the remaining two screws.

Many of the Activities require the valves to be free rather than fastened down on the baseboards. While the cylinders may be kept permanently mounted on the boards, the valves should only be screwed down when necessary.

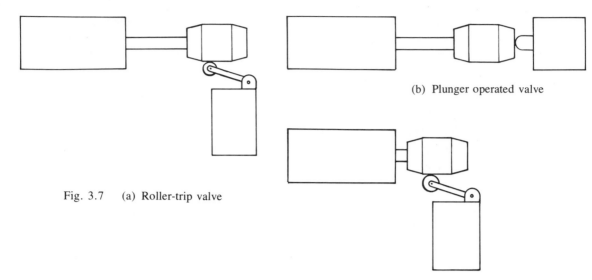

(b) Plunger operated valve

Fig. 3.7   (a) Roller-trip valve

Economatics retail a Hybridex-based component mounting system. Components are mounted on acrylic bases which are quickly attached to the Hybridex rails by four screwdriver operated spring-loaded fixings. The system is intended to be used to hold equipment in all the Activities. It incorporates a busbar which greatly simplifies multiple connections to the main air supply. The mounting system is a great convenience in practical work and enables circuits to be far tidier than when equipment is loose on a bench top. However, it does increase equipment costs, and wholly satisfactory work can be done with equipment loose on a bench top or mounted as required by the home-made methods described.

In order to minimise the initial cost of equipment for this module, the content of the kit has been pared to the absolute minimum consistent with a worthwhile course. The leanness of the equipment provision will be felt particularly in Activities 8 and 9 where, if no additional equipment is available, the number of working groups must be reduced from six to three. The experience of schools where this module has been taught for some time is that this situation is soon eased by the acquisition of scrap, but serviceable, equipment from industry. However, until such equipment is acquired, a way round the problem is to set three of the six groups former examination questions while the other three groups tackle the Activities. The following lesson, the groups change over.

The air-operated counter is a useful device, especially for project work, though it is much more expensive than its electromechanical equivalent. The counter's case is rather flimsy, but the unit is easily mounted in a strong enclosure and this should be done before the course commences. The counter is supplied with a small plug-in adaptor with a short length of nylon tube. If required, the adaptor can be removed from the counter by pressing down with a thumb nail or small screwdriver the brass ring through which the adaptor passes into the counter. The other end of the counter's nylon tube should be equipped with a Plasticon tubing nut assembly. If a counter with a much more robust casing is required, the more costly unit manufactured by Martonair (part number PS/615) is recommended. This can be supplied by Economatics as an alternative to the Crouzet counter when ordering the kit, or it can be obtained directly from Martonair.

Many equipment suppliers have a minimum order charge which can make it very difficult for a school to obtain a few low cost components. In order to assist schools, Economatics are willing to process small orders on a 'cash with order' plus postage and packing charge basis. Before placing an order, enquiry should be made of the prevailing terms of business and the threshold below which 'cash with order' applies. Other firms may well be willing to do business on a similar basis.

Equipment Expansion

This may well be a matter of seeing what surplus industrial equipment turns up rather than a planned program based on dependable financial resources! If purchasing is possible, one approach is to see what valves and cylinders become tied up in examination project work (and therefore unavailable when teaching the module) and buy duplicates. It is improbable that this would amount to another complete kit!

Another approach is to aim to purchase over a period of time duplicates of all the equipment required for Activities 8 and 9. This would ease a particularly tight spot in the practical work.

A duplicate of any piece of equipment in the kit is useful, except perhaps the counter. Of equipment not in the kit, a most useful item to have is a lever set/reset 3-port valve. Placed in an appropriate pilot line in automatic circuits, it provides the best means by which such circuits can be stopped and started. Its use is easily incorporated in the assignments.

Where surplus industrial equipment is concerned, it is an easy matter to write additional assignments, making use of the devices, to be carried out at an appropriate place in the course.

Additional Equipment Required for the Air Jet Devices and Logic Circuits Option

Quantity	Description	Part No.	Manufacturer/ Supplier
2	Emitter	4JS-030-000	
3	Touch sensor	4TS-010	
1	Impacting jet sensor	4JS-020-000	
1	Proximity sensor	4PS-910	
1	OR-NOR module (3-input)	4NR-201-000	
4	LP Boostermite	5BV-913	
1	Pressure regulator (0–7 bar)	11-990-006	IMI Norgren
1	Pressure gauge (0–1.6 bar)	18-013-991	
1	Miniature filter	F39-100-MOTG	
6	Cross-piece	P0152A-03	
10	Connector UNF to $1/16''$ i.d. tube	P0009A-03	
19	Connector UNF to $1/8''$ i.d. tube	P0010A-03	
1	Bleed connector	4TC-010	
6	Plug	P9037A-03	
4	Bulkhead connector, $1/8''$ BSP female to UNF	4BC-910	
6	Connector, $1/8''$ BSP to UNF	P9036A-03E	
17	Plasticon port adaptor, $1/8''$ BSP to 5 mm o.d. nylon tube	3030611	GKN Screws and Fasteners
3 m	$1/16''$ i.d. tube	P9018A-01	Economatics
3 m	$1/8''$ i.d. tube	P9019A-01	

Economatics can supply all the above items as a kit. Order as 'Econ. 269 Air Jet

Devices and Logic Circuits Option Kit'. Note the use of imperial units as this equipment is of American origin.

In addition to the above, a check unit with a ⅛'' BSP female threaded plug-in adaptor, and also a tee-piece, may be required in order to supply air for this equipment. Precise details depend on the particular air supply installation.

A supply of oil-free air is essential for this option. It can be obtained from the main high pressure system. Air from this system will have already passed through a filter and regulator. Provided these devices are *not followed by a lubricator*, the low pressure filter and regulator system can be connected directly to the high pressure system via a check unit. The additional filter is necessary because, while the air has not been through a lubricator, it may nevertheless carry traces of oil from the compressor's sump. This oil will clog the fine airways in the low pressure equipment.

If the high pressure air supply is lubricated, an oil-free supply can be obtained by installing a tee-piece after the filter and regulator, and before the lubricator. This branch should terminate in a check unit of a type different from that used for the high pressure supply. The check unit plug should have a ⅛'' BSP female thread into which a Plasticon port adaptor, ⅛'' BSP to 5 mm o.d. nylon tube, can be screwed.

The oil-free air passes from the check unit to the miniature filter through a nylon tube. This should be a clean one kept specially for this purpose. The miniature filter ports should be fitted with Plasticon port adaptors, ⅛'' BSP to 5 mm o.d. nylon tube. Note carefully which port is input and which is output.

Air from the miniature filter passes to the regulator and pressure gauge through a nylon tube. This connection can be permanent. The regulator ports should be fitted with Plasticon port adaptors ⅛'' BSP to 5 mm o.d. nylon tube. Note carefully the direction of the air flow through the regulator. This is indicated by an arrow on the bottom of the regulator body. The pressure gauge should be screwed into the appropriate port of the regulator, the gauge threads being first bound with PTFE tape. The regulator has two gauge ports. A blanking plug is provided for the unused port. Bind the plug's threads with PTFE tape.

Teachers are advised to mount the filter/regulator unit so that it is safe from accidental damage.

So that each of four groups of pupils can conveniently connect a circuit, one at a time, to the oil-free air supply, four adaptors must be assembled, one for each group. The adaptor is made up from a Plasticon port adaptor, ⅛'' BSP to 5 mm o.d. nylon tube, a bulkhead connector ⅛''·BSP to UNF and a connector UNF to ⅛'' i.d. tube (Fig. 3.8). A nylon tube is used to connect the adaptor to the filter/regulator unit. This tube should be a clean one kept specifically for this purpose.

Fig. 3.8

(a) Port adaptor, ⅛'' BSP to 5 mm o.d. nylon tube

(b) Bulkhead connector 10–32 UNF female × ⅛'' BSPT female – 4BC-910

(c) Connector 10–32 UNF male to ⅛'' i.d. flexible tubing – P0010A-03

All the main components are supplied boxed and with individual instructions. The sensing and Boostermite devices are supplied with a connector UNF to $\frac{1}{16}$'' and/or $\frac{1}{8}$'' i.d. tube. Care should be taken to follow the instructions and insert the connectors in the correct ports. Except for the touch sensors, the air supply to a device is via a UNF to $\frac{1}{8}$'' i.d. tube connector, while the air signal to or from a device is via a UNF to $\frac{1}{16}$'' i.d. tube connector. The touch sensors use two UNF to $\frac{1}{16}$'' i.d. tube connectors.

The Boostermite high pressure input and output ports must be equipped with Plasticon port adaptors, $\frac{1}{8}$'' BSP to 5 mm o.d. nylon tube. The Boostermite used in Activity 11 to receive the signal from the 3-input OR-NOR module must have its UNF to $\frac{1}{16}$'' i.d. tube connector exchanged for a bleed connector. (Fig. 3.9). This red coloured component is similar to the UNF to $\frac{1}{16}$'' i.d. tube connector but it has a small air bleed hole drilled in it. This ensures that, when the OR-NOR module stops signalling the Boostermite, the air pressure in the interconnecting tube decays rapidly. Were the bleed connector not there, the only way the air pressure could decay would be by an air flow back through the OR-NOR module, as there is no vent to atmosphere from the Boostermite's operating diaphragm.

Fig. 3.9   Bleed connector (coloured red) UNF to $\frac{1}{16}$'' i.d. tube

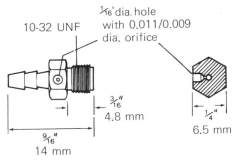

The $\frac{1}{8}$'' and $\frac{1}{16}$'' i.d. tube should be cut to provide sufficient lengths for an Activity. Lengths of about 300 m will be found convenient for most purposes. The tubes are not easily removed from their connectors and care must be taken to avoid damage when doing this. The problem eases when the inside ends of the tubes become worn. However, the problem can be avoided by not pushing the tubes over the connectors' shoulders, or by removing the sharp edge from the shoulders.

Three flow regulators from the main kit are required for this option. Remove the Plasticon port adaptors from them and replace each one with connector P9036A-03E ($\frac{1}{8}$'' BSPT to UNF) into which connector P0010A-03(UNF to $\frac{1}{8}$'' tube) has been fitted (Fig. 3.10)

Fig. 3.10   (a) Connector $\frac{1}{8}$'' BSPT male   (b) Connector 10–32 UNF male
                     × 10–32 UNF female   to $\frac{1}{8}$'' i.d. flexible tubing –
                     – P9036A-03E   P0010A-03

Prior to undertaking this option, various tees and connectors should be assembled and permanently numbered as indicated below. These are referred to by their numbers in the Workbook assignments. To make the tees and connectors, the six cross-pieces are fitted with 1/16'' and 1/8'' i.d. tube connectors and plugs according to Fig. 3.11.

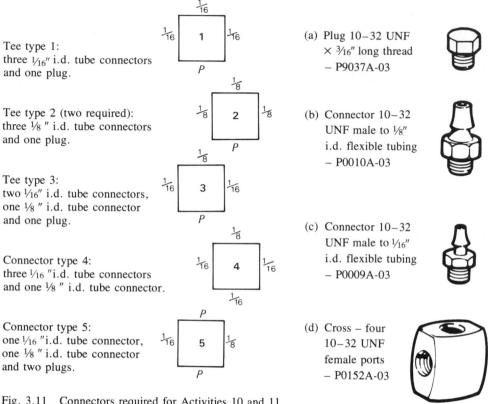

Tee type 1:
three 1/16'' i.d. tube connectors and one plug.

Tee type 2 (two required):
three 1/8'' i.d. tube connectors and one plug.

Tee type 3:
two 1/16'' i.d. tube connectors, one 1/8'' i.d. tube connector and one plug.

Connector type 4:
three 1/16'' i.d. tube connectors and one 1/8'' i.d. tube connector.

Connector type 5:
one 1/16'' i.d. tube connector, one 1/8'' i.d. tube connector and two plugs.

(a) Plug 10–32 UNF
× 3/16'' long thread
– P9037A-03

(b) Connector 10–32
UNF male to 1/8''
i.d. flexible tubing
– P0010A-03

(c) Connector 10–32
UNF male to 1/16''
i.d. flexible tubing
– P0009A-03

(d) Cross – four
10–32 UNF
female ports
– P0152A-03

Fig. 3.11   Connectors required for Activities 10 and 11

In Activity 10 and Activity 11 there is an assignment which requires a collector. This is readily made by the teacher to the details given in Fig. 3.12. Aluminium is the suggested material, although another metal or a plastic may be used instead.

Fig. 3.12   Collector required for Activities 10 and 11

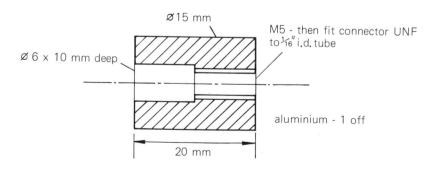

Ø15 mm

M5 - then fit connector UNF
to 1/16'' i.d. tube

Ø 6 x 10 mm deep

aluminium - 1 off

20 mm

Note that in Activity 11, Assignment 4, valves *B*, *C*, *D*, *E* and *F* require a Plasticon ⅛'' BSP to 5 mm o.d. nylon tube port adaptor in their exhaust ports, port number 3.

Connections to the OR-NOR module are made by pushing lengths of the $1/16'$ i.d. tube over the port spigots on the back of the module. The module manufacturers, IMI Norgren Ltd, produce sub-base units into which logic modules can be plugged. The $1/16''$ i.d. tubes are attached to the sub-base unit with UNF to $1/16''$ tube connectors. Logic modules can be changed at will without disturbing the tubing connections. If extra logic modules are purchased at some future date it is desirable to purchase with them some single or double sub-base units.

Fig. 3.13   Decision making system symbol for OR-NOR module

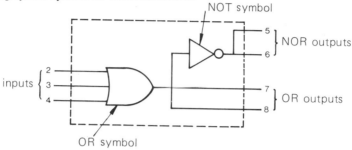

Figure 3.13 shows the decision making system symbols for the OR-NOR module. An input signal at port 2 OR 3 OR 4, or any combination of the three, causes an output from ports 7 and 8. This is the 'OR' function. If there is no signal at any of the three input ports then there is no output from ports 7 and 8.

When an input signal is present at port 2 OR 3 OR 4, or any combination of the three, there is NOT an output signal from ports 5 and 6. This is the 'NOR' (NOT OR) function. If there is no signal at any of the three input ports then there is an output from ports 5 and 6. Note that if only one input is used, together with a 'NOR' output, the device behaves as an inverter and performs the 'NOT' function.

The interrelationship of the high and low pressure air systems is summarised in Fig. 3.14.

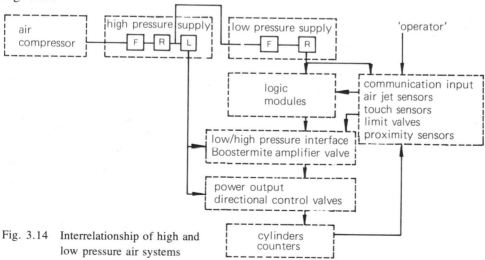

Fig. 3.14   Interrelationship of high and low pressure air systems

41

Equipment Expansion

IMI Norgren manufacture a range of fluid logic (fluidic) modules similar to the 3-input OR-NOR module. It is highly recommended that, as opportunity permits, this course option be expanded by the purchase of further modules. The following are suggested:

OR-NOR module   4NR-201-000 – this is additional to the module in the kit. All logic functions can be obtained by suitably interconnecting sufficient 'NOR' systems or by purchasing the following.

AND-NAND module   4AN-203-000
FLIP-FLOP module   4FF-202-000
EXCLUSIVE-OR module   4XR-208-000.

The modules can be used on their own to demonstrate basic logic functions, and in combination to fulfil more complex control requirements. Electronic integrated circuits are more frequently used in logic control systems. However, for teaching the fundamentals of logic systems, fluid logic devices are convenient, quick to interconnect and virtually proof against damage caused by misconnection and inexperience.

Fig. 3.15   Decision making system symbols for AND-NAND module

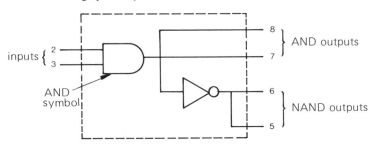

Figure 3.15 gives the decision making system symbols for the AND-NAND module. When input signals are present at both port 2 AND port 3 there is an output from ports 7 and 8. This is the 'AND' function. If either or both of the input signals at ports 2 and 3 are absent there is no output from ports 7 and 8.

When input signals are present at both port 2 AND port 3 there is NOT an output from ports 5 and 6. This is the 'NAND' ('NOT AND') function. If either or both of the input signals at ports 2 and 3 are absent, there is an output from ports 5 and 6.

Note that if both inputs are T-connected together and a 'NAND' output is used, the device behaves as an inverter and performs the 'NOT' function.

Fig. 3.16   Decision making system symbols for FLIP-FLOP module

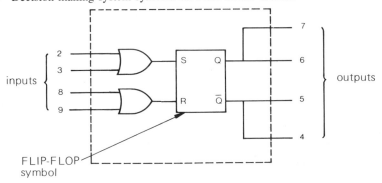

42

Figure 3.16 gives the decision making system symbols for the FLIP-FLOP module. A momentary signal at input port 2 OR 3 is the set signal. This turns on the Q output which is continuously available at output ports 6 and 7. A momentary signal at input port 8 OR 9 is the reset signal. This turns off the Q output from ports 6 and 7. A $\overline{Q}$ (NOT Q) output is available at ports 4 and 5. The $\overline{Q}$ output is always the opposite of the Q output. Either or both of the outputs Q and $\overline{Q}$ can be used according to the situation in hand.

Fig. 3.17   Decision making system symbols for EXCLUSIVE-OR module

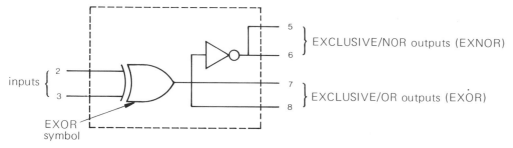

Figure 3.17 gives the decision making system symbols for the EXCLUSIVE-OR module. There are two ways of understanding this module.

1   An input signal at port 2 OR port 3 but not both at the same time (this possibility is excluded) causes an output to be available at ports 7 and 8. This is the EXCLUSIVE-OR function (EXOR). If inputs 2 and 3 are both on or both off, then there is no output from ports 7 and 8.

An input signal at port 2 OR port 3 but not both at the same time causes an output NOT to be available at ports 5 and 6. This is the EXCLUSIVE-NOR function (EXNOR). If inputs 2 and 3 are both on or both off, then there is an output from ports 5 and 6.

2   This module can be used as a comparator. It compares the input signals at ports 2 and 3. If they are the same (both on or both off) the module gives an output at ports 5 and 6 (EXNOR). The output at ports 7 and 8 is off. If the inputs are different, the module gives an output at ports 7 and 8 (EXOR). The output at ports 5 and 6 is off.

In all cases, the output(s) used depends on the situation being dealt with.

Assignments should be written to demonstrate these modules. Additional assignments which require the modules to be used in combination can be devised. These will prove a stimulating challenge for even the most able pupils. Circuit diagram drawing, decision-making system symbol drawing and truth table compilation should be included in the work. Inspiration for assignment writing, as well as application examples, can be found in 'A Guide to Practical Fluidic Circuits', a booklet produced by IMI Norgren Ltd. This should be read along with their 'Introduction to Digital Fluidics' and their 'Fluidic Product Review'. Further help may be obtained from the many digital electronic 'Teach-in' series published in electronic magazines and from the many introductory books on the same subject. The symbols and logic functions are directly transferable from electronics to fluidics. Only the hardware differs: it uses fluid flow rather than electron flow. Consultation with the mathematics/computer studies department may be helpful in evolving assignments. There may be differences of opinion on the logic symbols used! Those given here are American in origin and are the most widely used. However, be aware of the British Standard symbols in BS 3939, any changes in general usage, Examination Board requirements, and respond appropriately.

In addition to the modules listed, a number of other input sensors is available together with output devices which include visual indicators (the 'Rotowink') and an electrical switch which is actuated by a very low pressure air signal.

Although they are not used in the text, teachers may find it useful to be aware of some further general logic symbols which are widely used. The symbols are for NOR, NAND and EXNOR. In the text these are shown as OR followed by NOT, AND followed by NOT and EXOR followed by NOT. Each pair of symbols can be conflated to give the single symbols shown in Fig. 3.18. The little circle on each single symbol indicates a negated output.

Fig. 3.18   Symbols for NOR, NAND and EXNOR

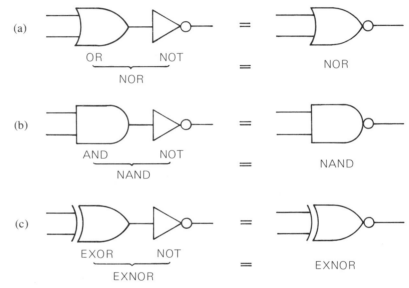

The single symbol can represent the function of a single, specialised two (or more) input device. Alternatively, if one wishes, it can represent the combined effect of two separate devices.

Just as outputs can be negated, inputs can be negated too. Some examples are shown in Fig. 3.19.

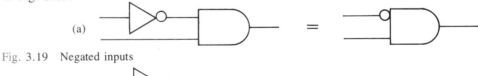

Fig. 3.19   Negated inputs

As before, the single symbol can represent the function of a single specialised device. It can also represent the combined effect of separate devices. Systems such as these can be investigated in practical work assignments.

44

4 Compressors, Receivers and Air Lines

Compressed air is stored energy. This stored energy can be used to do work when the air is supplied to a pneumatic cylinder. The pressure of the air acting on the surface area of the piston generates a force. When the force is applied to a load which then moves through a distance, work is done.

In the compressor, mechanical work is done on the air in order to compress it. The compressor therefore requires an energy input. With a bicycle or car pump, a human being provides the energy input to the pump piston for it to do mechanical work. The origins of that energy can be traced through a complex chain of conversions of which human metabolism is one of the latest. A compressor is usually driven by an electric motor or internal combustion engine. After complex conversions, the energy for these power units arrives in electrical or chemical form. By further conversions through magnetic or heat forms within the power units, a mechanical energy input is available to the compressor. Here the chain of energy conversions – with all their attendant losses – continues as air is compressed and made available to do work. Pupils should be made aware of these energy conversion chains.

Fig. 4.1   A simple compressor unit

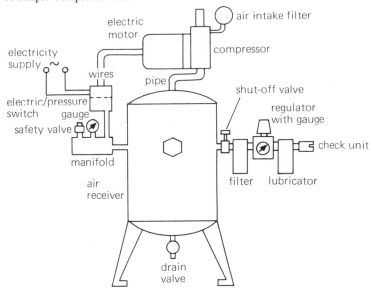

45

Starting with the pneumatic valves and cylinders and working back through the system, the supplying of compressed air can be considered in four parts.

1   Conveying the compressed air to the pneumatic components – the air line.
2   Conditioning the compressed air – the removal of dust, dirt and water vapour and lubrication of the air.
3   Storing the compressed air to provide a constant supply – the receiver and the compressor control system.
4   Producing compressed air – the compressor and its power unit.

Figure 4.1 details the essential features of a simple compressed air supply system, while Fig. 4.2 illustrates this using standard symbols.

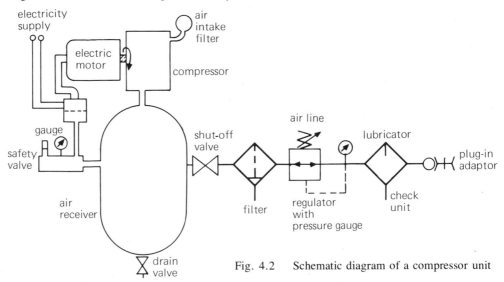

Fig. 4.2   Schematic diagram of a compressor unit

Fig. 4.3   Simple air line circuit for a school workshop

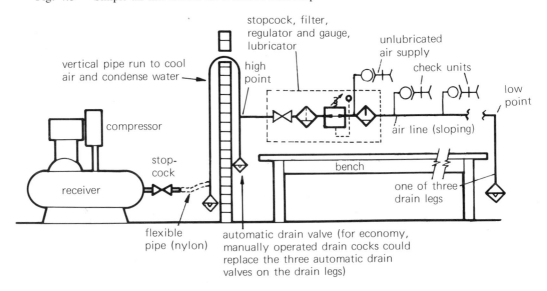

46

1 The Air Line

The main air supply pipe around a workshop is called an air line. It must be stressed that an air line is highly desirable for, but by no means essential to, this course. A small, free-standing compressor with one outlet can be used. This is not as convenient as an air line and will soon 'run out of breath', although it does get the course going and can be replaced in due time.

Figure 4.3 summarises the essential features for a school air line and should be closely studied. The pipe is ½'' (12½ mm) bore galvanised steel water pipe. It is laid with a slight slope, the point of entry of the air from the compressor being at the highest point. At the lowest point, a short, vertical length of pipe is fitted and equipped with a drain valve. This forms a drain leg and allows condensate to be removed. Other drain legs are required at other points in the system. In a large installation in a factory or garage, it is usual to have a ring main air line (Fig. 4.4). This has the advantage of having no dead ends. The closed circuit provides instant air supply to all the connection points round the circular line.

Fig. 4.4   Ring main for a factory or garage

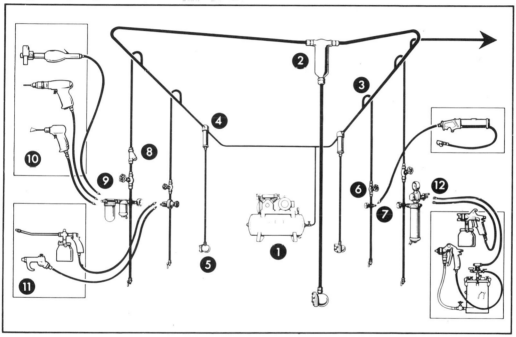

1 compressor 2 moisture trap 3 individual take-off points 4 filter/moisture separator 5 automatic drain 6 isolating wheel valve 7 Instantair bayonet connection 8 solids separator 9 moisture separator/lubricator 10 percussion tools, drills, grinders etc. 11 blow guns, oil/water guns 12 moisture separator/reducing valve, for spray guns.

Pipe fittings, such as elbows, tees and bends, all ½'' BSP, are used to produce corners and junctions in the air line. The fittings should be kept to a minimum as they cause air flow resistance and hence create a pressure loss in the air line. Screw fittings should be sealed with jointing compound or PTFE sealant tape. The pipework should be tested for leaks. One method of doing this is to paint the joints with a solution of soapy water, so that any air leaks will produce bubbles. An alternative method is to turn on the compressed air and then seal off the supply, and note whether the pressure falls in a ten-minute period.

The compressor unit is connected to the air line by a length of flexible nylon pipe. This prevents compressor vibration travelling along the air line.

Pneumatic circuits are connected to the air line by means of check units and plug-in adaptors. Various models are available from different suppliers, Martonair (Fig. 4.5a), BroomWade (Fig. 4.5b) and Schrader (Fig. 3.4) for example. A tee-piece is installed in an air line where an air outlet is required. The tee is set in the air line so that air has to rise vertically from the air line. This avoids the carry over of condensate to the pneumatic equipment. An elbow screwed into the tee-piece allows the check unit to lie horizontally for easy access. Where high pressure lubricated and low pressure unlubricated air supplies are both available, different types of check unit and plug-in adaptor should be used for each supply system.

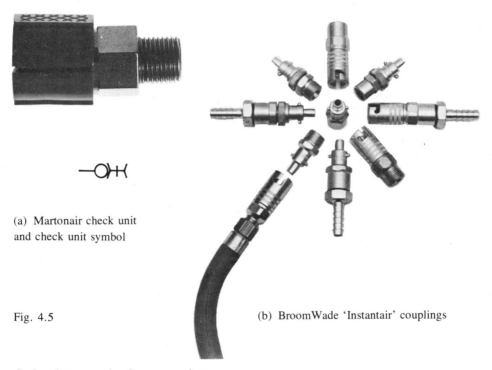

(a) Martonair check unit and check unit symbol

Fig. 4.5

(b) BroomWade 'Instantair' couplings

2 Conditioning the Compressed Air

Conditioning the supply of compressed air can be divided into four stages.

(a) Removing dust and dirt particles from the air intake to the compressor.

(b) Removing water from the compressed air.

(c) Regulating the air pressure to the level required by pneumatic equipment.

(d) Lubricating the air supplied to components.

Dust and dirt removal from the atmospheric intake air is usually achieved by putting an air filter on the compressor air intake (Figs. 4.1, 4.2 and 4.13). This filter is a metal canister containing a fibre gauze or a wire mesh. It screws directly into the air intake of the compressor cylinder. Dirt or dust can do a great deal of damage to the inside of cylinders and valves by scratching metal bores and wearing synthetic rubber and nylon seals.

While the majority of water vapour present in air when it is extracted from the atmosphere condenses in the air receiver, some remains and it is essential to remove as much as possible because of its corrosive action on the inside of cylinders and valves. This is done by filtering the air when it leaves the receiver (Fig. 4.6).

Fig. 4.6 (a) Filter with nylon element
(b) BSI/ISO symbol for filter

Initially, a filter relies on a centrifuging action. The compressed air enters the filter through a circular ring with small vanes beneath it. The swirling movement of the air causes dirt particles and water to be thrown against the filter walls. The compressed air then passes through a filter element with a fine mesh size (e.g. 64 microns). Filter elements constructed of sintered bronze, nylon, felt, paper, cotton or wire mesh are used. In some units, the filter element's need for cleaning is indicated when a coloured ring is obscured by a band on the filter bowl. The filter element is washed in a solvent such as paraffin or liquid detergent. Condensate which has accumulated in the filter bowl is removed through an automatic or manual drain valve at the base of the filter bowl.

The pressure of the air supplied to pneumatic components is substantially lower than the pressure of the air in the air receiver. The receiver may be at 8 bar or more, whereas a pressure of 6 bar or lower is suitable for operating the pneumatic components. In operation, the receiver pressure continually varies over a range of about 1 bar. These pressure fluctuations have no effect on the air line pressure. A pressure regulator is a device which can give a stable pressure output of any required value lower than a variable pressure input. A pressure gauge can be screwed into a regulator to indicate the output pressure (Fig. 4.7).

Fig. 4.7   (a) Regulator with gauge   (b) BSI/ISO symbol for regulator with gauge

A pressure regulator is fitted in the air line after the filter. There are two main types of regulator, relieving and non-relieving. A relieving regulator allows the air line pressure to be immediately reduced from a high value to a lower value as the regulator vents the excess air in the line to atmosphere. This does not happen with a non-relieving regulator. The regulator may be readjusted to give a lower line pressure, but this pressure will only be obtained when the excess air has been used by pneumatic equipment or vented to atmosphere by opening a check unit. A relieving regulator is preferable. Sectioned diagrams and explanations of the operation of a regulator are to be found in equipment manufacturers' catalogues.

The most effective method of lubricating pneumatic components such as cylinders and valves is to use an airborne lubricant. A fine mist or fog of oil in the air will reach the moving parts of the components. A lubricator unit introduces this oil into the passing air flow. The lubricator is placed in the air line after the pressure regulator. Figure 4.8 shows an 'oil mist' type of lubricator. This injects a very fine mist of oil into the air stream through a jet. Care must be taken when choosing a lubricator. Some lubricators will not function when the rate of air flow is low. Also, if the rate of flow is low and the pipe run long, large droplets of oil are deposited in the air line and do not reach the equipment. For low air flow rates a 'micro oil fog' lubricator should be used and is best suited to the operating conditions of school pneumatics. A lubricator is not absolutely essential to a small system in school which uses a portable compressor unit. Cylinders and valves can be given an occasional drop of light oil, e.g. 'Three-in-one'. However a lubricator should be included in a permanent air line system and filled with a thin oil such as Shell Tellus 21 or 27.

Fig. 4.8   (a) Lubricator unit

(b) BSI/ISO symbol for lubricator

Lubricators are *not* required for fluid logic or low pressure device circuits as there are no moving parts and there is a risk of blocking fine air ways with oil. To supply such devices, a tee-piece is installed after the regulator and before the lubricator so that the air line can be split into two branches. One branch supplies clean, dry air which will require further filtration and regulation before use in low pressure circuits, while the other branch passes air to the lubricator for treatment.

An air compressor as supplied by a manufacturer is not equipped with any means of conditioning the compressed air before use in pneumatic equipment. A filter, regulator and gauge, and a lubricator must be purchased separately. A large range of these devices is available. The main factor to consider in making a choice is the maximum rate of air flow likely to be demanded at any given instant, rather than the maximum average rate of flow per minute. Equipment catalogues can give helpful guidance on appropriate devices, while personal contact with a supplier's representative can remove doubts as to which items in their range are best suited to a particular installation. The compressor's manufacturer may also be able to supply this service.

Fig. 4.9   (a) 'Olympian' system filter, regulator, gauge and lubricator unit

                (b) Circuit diagram symbol for a combined
                      filter, regulator and lubricator unit

         (c) Individual components of the system
             shown in (a)

lubricator

filter

regulator
with
gauge

Individual filters, regulators and lubricators, such as those shown in Figs. 4.6, 4.7 and 4.8, are best connected together with flat unions. The units are then easy to remove from the air line if necessary. When connecting the devices, ensure that the direction of air flow through each unit is correct. Flow direction is usually indicated by an arrow on the body of the device. Some manufacturers have available 'off the shelf' pre-assembled sets of three matching devices.

Specially recommended is the 'Olympian' range of compressed air conditioning units manufactured by IMI Norgren Ltd (Fig. 4.9a and c). Each unit is held in a mounting yoke by a locking ring. The locking ring is unscrewed manually to release the unit from the yoke. This system is particularly advantageous when building an air line on a 'do-it-yourself' basis. The required number of yokes and other components can be assembled and fixed to a wall, and the pipes then attached prior to the insertion of the conditioning units. Correct positioning and pipe lengths are assured, and the risk of damage to the conditioning units is avoided. Full details of the system can be obtained from the manufacturer. A system made up from the 'Olympian' range and used successfully with a 9 cfm (4.2 litre/s) compressor supplying six check units is shown in Fig. 4.9a. The individual components which comprise the system are shown in Fig. 4.9c and are as listed below.

1	Shut-off valve, ½'' BSPP end connector	T13-400-E2AD
2	Yoke (single)	5224-95
1	Porting block kit, ¼'' BSPT port	18-026-992
1	Wall mounting kit	18-001-987
1	Yoke connecting kit	18-026-996
1	Insert, ½'' BSPP	5223-71
1	Pack of 20 retaining pins	2378-97
1	Filter regulator, manual drain	B13-000-M3MO
1	Lubricator, micro-fog type	L13-000-MPEO
1	Pressure gauge, 0-11 bar	18-013-013
1	Plug, ¼'' BSPT	

Inclusion of the porting block makes it a simple matter to obtain oil-free air for the 'Air Jet Devices and Logic Circuits' option in the module. The plug in the porting block is removed and a Plasticon port adaptor, ¼'' BSP to 8 mm o.d. nylon tube, installed. Connection is then made by 8 mm nylon tube to a suitable wall-mounted check unit. This should be of a type different from that used for lubricated air, so that the risk of incorrect connection of low pressure, oil-free equipment is minimised.

Note that where a small portable air compressor is used with conditioning units directly screwed to the air receiver, one or two check units with plug-in adaptors may also have to be purchased along with the conditioning units. If two check units are required, a tee-piece will be needed to supply them both.

3 Receivers

An air receiver is a pressure vessel designed to store compressed air until it is required for use. In a small compressor unit, the compressor is mounted on top of a vertical or horizontal air receiver (Figs. 4.13 and 4.14). The receiver is a cylindrical steel container of welded construction made from low carbon steel plate. A pressure vessel like a receiver has to be hydraulically tested by a competent engineer and clearly marked with the safe working pressure (SWP). If not already done, the SWP should be painted on the receiver so that it is quite obvious. The actual value will be on an inspection plate on the machine, impressed in the end of the receiver and written in the machine's inspection documents. If a secondhand machine has been obtained it is just possible that its SWP may have been down-rated at some time. This should be ascertained, and in any case the machine must be inspected by the insurance company's engineer before being used. The Factories Act requires pressure vessels to be inspected every twenty-six months (see Section 5 on safety). An air receiver has at least one inspection cap. This is a screw cap (50 mm minimum diameter) which can be unscrewed with a large spanner to allow the inside of the receiver to be inspected for corrosion. Only commercially made receivers should be used for compressor units. Improvised receivers should *never* be used because of the risk of explosion.

Atmospheric air contains water vapour, the amount depending on the temperature and volume of the air. An air compressor should take in the coolest air possible. This contains the least amount of water. It also has a greater density and therefore each stroke draws in a greater mass of air. If at all possible, the compressor chamber should be directly ventilated by air from outside the building. When the air is compressed its volume decreases, but because its temperature has risen it is still able to hold its water vapour. After compression the air passes into the receiver and cools down. The water vapour now condenses and collects at the bottom of the receiver. All receivers must be fitted with a drain valve at their lowest point so that the condensate can be drained away. Large compressors have an automatic drain valve and require no attention other than routine maintenance checks. Smaller units have a manually operated drain valve which should be opened regularly – say, weekly, with school usage of the compressor. If the drain valve is opened when the receiver still has a very low residual air pressure, water is easily driven out and can be collected in a container or absorbed by sawdust.

The pressure of compressed air inside a receiver is indicated by a Bourdon pressure gauge on the receiver (Fig. 4.13). The air receiver must be fitted with a safety relief valve which can be set at a pre-determined pressure below the safe working pressure. If the preset pressure is exceeded, the safety relief valve (Fig. 4.10) lifts and releases the compressed air to atmosphere. The pop safety relief valve is fitted with a plunger with a knob on the top or a hole for inserting a ring to enable the ball inside to be lifted off its seat manually for test purposes.

Fig. 4.10   Pop safety relief valve – adjustable

Many receivers are also fitted with a safety relief valve (Fig. 4.11). This is fitted with a strong spring, the loading of which is adjusted by the knurled screw on top of the valve. If excessive air pressure builds up, it overcomes the spring loading and lifts the valve, allowing the compressed air to vent to atmosphere through a hole at the top of the valve. A stop/start pressure (or regulator) switch is essential on a compressor unit (see Fig. 4.1). The mains electrical supply to the motor is connected through this switch on small compressors. Larger units have a separate starter, as the motor current is too large to be handled by the contacts of a pressure switch. This switch makes and breaks the

Fig. 4.11   Safety relief valve and symbol

supply to the starter solenoid coil. The current which operates the solenoid coil is very small, normally only a few milliamps. The pressure of the air in the receiver acts on a diaphragm in the pressure switch. Movement of the diaphragm, due to air pressure changes, switches the electricity supply to the motor on or off. If the pressure in the receiver falls below a minimum value, say 7 bar, the motor is automatically turned on. When the receiver air pressure rises to a maximum value, say 8 bar, the electric motor is turned off. The pressure switch is usually fitted with a manual on/off switch for shutting down the system after use or turning it on for an operating session. A relief valve isolates the compressor from the high pressure air in the receiver when the electric motor is turned off. This ensures that the motor does not restart with the full pressure load of the air receiver on the piston of the compressor. If the motor was continually started under the pressure load of a full air receiver, there would be an excessive initial current flow and possible motor stalling and burn out. *It is therefore essential that this switch is always used to stop or start the compressor.*

4 Compressors
A compressor is a pump which compresses a large volume of free atmospheric air into a small enclosed volume and so raises the pressure of the air. Compressors can be classified into five types:
(a) reciprocating (piston)
(b) centrifugal
(c) rotary vane
(d) rotary screw
(e) turbine

(a) Reciprocating compressors
In a reciprocating compressor, a piston moving backwards and forwards in a cylinder compresses the air. A reciprocating compressor with one or more cylinders of equal size is called a single stage compressor (Fig. 4.12a). A two-stage compressor (Fig. 4.12b) has cylinders of different diameters, the larger one being the low pressure cylinder and the smaller the high pressure cylinder. Air is first compressed in the low pressure cylinder and then passed to the high pressure cylinder for further compression. Compressors with three or more cylinders of unequal sizes are normally called multi-stage units.

When air is compressed in each cylinder, its temperature rises. To remove as much of this heat as possible in two-stage and multi-stage machines, intercoolers are fitted. The compressed air from each cylinder is passed through an intercooler before further compression in the next stage.

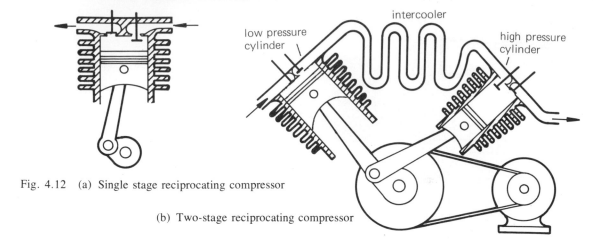

Fig. 4.12   (a) Single stage reciprocating compressor

(b) Two-stage reciprocating compressor

Single stage reciprocating compressors are suitable for producing air pressures of up to 10 bar. Two-stage reciprocating compressors are used for pressures of up to 40 bar. Multi-stage compressors can produce pressures as high as 1000 bar. For most pneumatic applications pressures up to 10 bar are sufficient.

Single phase electric motors are used to drive small single stage compressors (Fig. 4.13). Three-phase electric motors with pulley and belt speed reduction (and hence torque increase) are used for larger two-stage reciprocating compressors (Fig. 4.14).

Fig. 4.13   Single stage reciprocating compressor (with vertical receiver)

Fig. 4.14 Two-stage reciprocating compressor (with horizontal receiver)

The size of a compressor is often given by the manufacturer in litres per second (or cubic feet per minute) 'displacement'. This is not the actual output of the machine but the volume swept by the first stage piston each second (or minute). The actual output is expressed as litres per second (or cubic feet per minute) 'free air delivered'. As no compressor is one hundred per cent efficient, this figure will always be less than the displacement, and is a true measure of the actual amount of air obtainable from the compressor. Examples of compressor displacement for a range of BroomeWade compressors are shown in the table below. These are all single stage compressors suitable for school use.

A Range of BroomWade Compressors

Model	Displacement		Maximum Delivery Pressure		Motor	
	cfm	litre/s	psi.g	bar	HP	kW
Verticair	2.60	1.20	120	8.3	0.50	0.37
2003H	2.93	1.38	125	8.5	0.75	0.56
2004H	4.50	2.12	125	8.5	1.00	0.75
2006H	5.86	2.76	125	8.5	1.50	1.10
2009H	9.00	4.24	125	8.5	2.00	1.50
2015H	15.40	7.30	125	8.5	3.00	2.20
2030H	28.40	13.40	125	8.5	5.50	4.10
2050H	48.00	22.65	125	8.5	10.00	7.46

H indicates horizontal receiver.

Within a single stage compressor, a piston reciprocates in a cylinder, compressing air as it does so. As the piston moves in the cylinder through one cycle, from top dead centre to bottom dead centre and back to top dead centre, the volume of the cylinder changes.

As the cylinder volume changes, so does the volume of the gas within it. As the volume of the gas changes, its pressure and temperature change. As gas is discharged from the cylinder before top dead centre and enters the cylinder before bottom dead centre, the mass of gas in the cylinder is changing too. This also affects the pressure (and temperature) of the gas at any given volume in the cycle. These interacting factors are described by the gas laws (eg. Boyle's law, Charles' law) and are more easily appreciated graphically in an indicator diagram (Fig. 4.15). This diagram plots cylinder gas pressure against volume. The diagram is obtained by use of an instrument (an indicator) which reads directly from the cylinder during normal running. The diagram shows one complete cycle of the piston.

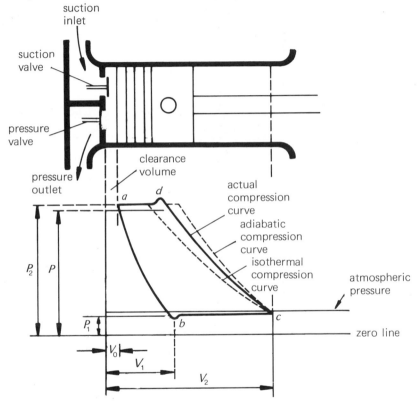

Fig. 4.15   Indicator diagram for a reciprocating compressor

Referring to Fig. 4.15, at the top dead centre of its stroke, the piston traps a clearance volume V_0 at pressure P_2 (point a). This is the delivery pressure of the previous piston stroke. As the piston moves down the cylinder, the air expands (line ab). The pressure falls below atmospheric pressure. When the suction valve opens (point b), air is drawn into the compressor cylinder chamber at pressure P_1 (line bc), until the piston reaches bottom dead centre (point c). The compression stroke (line cd) should ideally be isothermal, i.e. with no temperature rise. Teachers with a knowledge of thermodynamics will realise that the actual compression curve approaches the adiabatic curve, since the air temperature rises (see Fig. 4.15). The air receiver is at pressure P. When the cylinder air pressure rises above this value (point d), the pressure valve opens and air is forced into the receiver at delivery pressure P_2 (line da). The cycle then repeats.

58

In piston compressors, where the crankshaft and big-end bearings are running in lubricating oil, some oil inevitably gets past the scraper rings of the piston. This oil tends to form an emulsion with the water vapour in the compressed air. For pneumatic work this is not a major problem, but for some applications like food processing, brewing, chemical processing and instrumentation, clean dry air is essential. Special dry cylinder compressors are used for these applications (Fig. 4.16). These dry cylinder compressors have carbon rings and scraper glands.

Fig. 4.16   BroomWade dry cylinder compressor

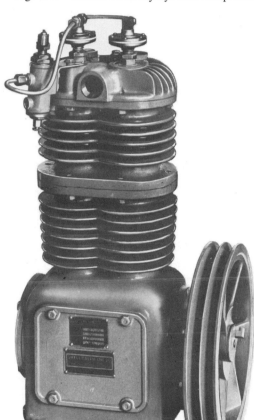

(b) Centrifugal compressors

The centrifugal compressor has a fast rotating fan at the centre of a spiral shaped case (Fig. 4.17). These compressors are used when low pressures and large displacement volumes of air are required, such as in dust extraction units. They are sometimes used as forge blowers. The central fan can be directly driven from an electric motor or an internal combustion engine. Fast fan speeds are possible since, in a centrifugal compressor, there are no valves which could stick or bounce. Centrifugal compressors are essentially 'blowers' and are not suitable for pneumatics.

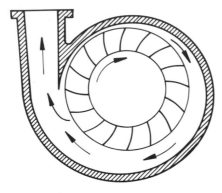
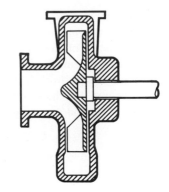

Fig. 4.17 Centrifugal compressor

(c) Rotating vane compressors

Rotating vane compressors have an eccentrically mounted rotor in which grooves have been machined (Fig. 4.18). Sliding vanes are positioned in the grooves of the rotor. Centrifugal action on the rotating vanes causes them to move outwards against the casing wall. The volume occupied by air between the vanes on the 'intake' side is large. Due to the eccentric mounting of the rotor, this volume decreases as the rotor turns and the vanes slide into the rotor grooves.

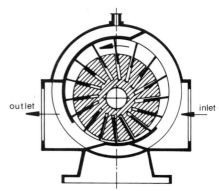

Fig. 4.18 Rotating vane compressor

As the volume of the air has decreased, its pressure (and temperature) have increased.

The rotating vane compressor is usually driven by a petrol or diesel engine although electric motors are sometimes used. High rotor speeds are possible because of the absence of valves which could stick or bounce at high operating speeds. Rotating vane compressors can produce higher pressures than centrifugal compressors, but not as high as the extremes attainable with piston compressors. For units of similar size, the volume of air produced in unit time by a rotating vane compressor is larger than a piston compressor, but not as large as a centrifugal compressor. Small rotating vane compressors are sometimes used for brazing hearth blowers. Large units are available for pneumatics and road repair work. They are more expensive than a reciprocating compressor of similar performance though they make less noise.

(d) Rotary screw compressors

Two multi-start screws, one left hand, the other right hand, rotate about parallel axes spaced so that the screws mesh with each other. The cross-sectional profiles of the screws are different. The thread, or lobes, on one look similar to the normal vee form; the other has spaces between the threads which are similar to the flutes of a twist drill (see Fig. 4.19). When meshed, there are spaces between the lobes and flutes but fine manufacturing clearances ensure that parallel spaces are sealed from each other. The spaces become smaller along the length of the screws. Thus, air entering the screws through an inlet port at one end is compressed as it passes along their length to be discharged through an outlet port.

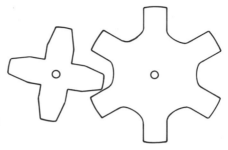

While these compressors offer substantial advantages over reciprocating compressors in industrial situations, even the smallest is too large and expensive for school use.

Fig. 4.19   End view of screws showing cross-sectional profile

(e) Turbine compressors

When very large volumes of air output are required, such as in mine ventilation, foundries and quarries, turbine compressors are used. They are often driven by diesel engines. Turbine compressors are an integral part of any jet or gas turbine engine where they supply a large volume of air under pressure to the combustion chambers.

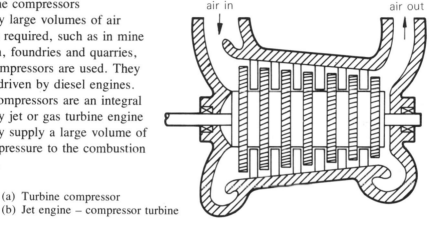

Fig. 4.20   (a) Turbine compressor
(b) Jet engine – compressor turbine

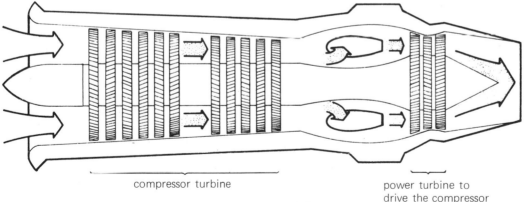

compressor turbine

power turbine to drive the compressor turbine

Choosing a Compressor Unit for a School

A single stage reciprocating compressor unit is suitable for school use. A wide choice of units varying in capacity and price is available. A few of these are shown in Fig. 4.21.

Fig. 4.21   A selection of BroomWade compressors

Fig. 4.22   Handiair 2

A very small unit is the portable Handiair 2 by BroomWade (Fig. 4.22). It has no air receiver and is only suitable for small pneumatic circuits, spraying and motor vehicle applications. A similar unit is the Handivac. This has a vacuum facility as well as supplying compressed air and thus is additionally useful for plastic forming and vacuum bag work in woodwork. These units can be mounted on an air receiver, and this arrangement represents the very minimum size of unit for supplying compressed air for the course. It can only be expected to supply one group of pupils at a time and will soon 'run out of breath' if connected to a large circuit. However, it will serve course purposes and is a useful, easy to move machine. Larger units such as models 2003H and 2004H in the BroomWade '2000 Series' can cope with several small circuits simultaneously or two sequential control circuits. Details of these machines are given in the table on page 57.

These units are not suitable for connection to a round-the-workshop air line. A filter, regulator and lubricator would be fitted to the receiver's outlet. These would be followed by a tee-piece and two check units so that two circuits can run simultaneously. Provided stability can be assured, the compressor can be mounted on wheels for easy movement to and from the working area. Small air compressors do not need to be permanently wired to an electricity supply but can be run from a 13 amp socket. However, it is essential that the compressor is always started and stopped at its pressure switch and not directly from the 13 amp socket.

Fig. 4.23   BroomWade Model 2050H compressor – large horizontal receiver

If a round-the-workshop air line is planned, a larger compressor unit is required. Model 2050H (Fig. 4.23) can supply air to several workshops for pneumatic and motor vehicle work, and is far larger than any but the most exceptional school circumstances will require. See the table on page 57 for details of this and other Broom Wade compressors.

A useful range of competitively priced compressors is manufactured by Clarkes Compressors Group. Details are given in the table below. These machines have horizontal air receivers and can be driven by single or three-phase electric motors, with the exception of Model 3A which requires a single phase motor.

Model	Displacement		Maximum Delivery Pressure		Motor	
	cfm	litre/s	psi.g	bar	HP	kW
SE/3A	3	1.41	115	7.9	0.66	0.49
SE/5A	5	2.35	150	10.3	1.00	0.75
SE7A	7	3.30	150	10.3	1.50	1.10
SE/9A	9	4.24	150	10.3	2.00	1.50
SE/14A	14	6.60	150	10.3	3.00	2.20

The ideal situation for teaching pneumatics is a workshop with a permanent air line supplied by the largest compressor possible. However a 9 cfm (4.2 litre/s) compressor feeding an air line with six check units has been found very satisfactory in the school pneumatics teaching situation. It copes with most demands, only 'running out of breath' when large sequential control circuits are connected to all six check units simultaneously. When this happens the only answer is for everyone to unplug and allow the machine to recover.

Low air supply pressure can be the cause of mysterious malfunctioning of correctly connected circuits. It is as well to check the pressure gauge before assuming that equipment is faulty. Apart from the compressor not being switched on, low air supply pressure can be caused by severe over-demand from the compressor as mentioned above. It can also be caused by a thermal trip in the electricity supply system cutting out the compressor's motor. This can happen because of a temperature rise in the compressor chamber or cupboard brought about by a prolonged period of near continuous running of the machine. The thermal trip is usually easily reset by operating the button or lever on the machine's contactor unit.

To minimise noise, the compressor should be outside the teaching area. Ideally it should be installed in an adjacent, secure, well ventilated and spacious outbuilding. This ensures minimum noise from, and adequate cooling of, the machine while allowing it to breathe the coolest air. Failing this, installation in a store room or spacious built-in cupboard will be satisfactory. It is essential that such a situation be well ventilated, preferably directly by the air outside the building. The compressor must be adequately cooled and it should breathe the coolest possible air. This increases the efficiency of the compressor, as a greater mass of air will be drawn in at each suction stroke.

A compressor chamber built in an open store area and placed against the brick wall which separates this area from the teaching area has proved satisfactory for a 9 cfm (4.2 litre/s) compressor running for lesson lengths of time. The material is 18 mm flooring grade chipboard laid on a deal frame. The dimensions are 1950 mm long × 1040 mm high × 900 mm deep. Access is through two removable half-length front panels. Ventilation to outside the building is via a 450 mm × 350 mm hole in the building wall. The hole is covered with expanded metal (loudspeaker grill), and a vee-hood on the outside prevents ingress of driving rain. While teachers must make arrangements which suit their particular circumstances, it is hoped that this brief account of a successful installation will prove a helpful starting point for some.

Compressors require little maintenance beyond an occasional wipe over and a check on the sump oil level. Top up with Shell 'Talpa 30' or whatever the manufacturer recommends.

Air Line Pressure

In industrial situations a regulator setting giving an air line pressure of 6 bar or more is likely. In the school situation it is recommended that 6 bar should not be exceeded. Indeed, a lower pressure setting is desirable, say 3 or 4 bar. From a safety angle, this reduces the magnitude of the forces generated by cylinders. From the practical point of view, far less compressed air is used, and the onset of 'breathlessness' in a heavily loaded compressor is considerably delayed. However, too low an air pressure will cause unreliable valve operation and may impair the action of the lubricator.

5 Safety

General Safety Recommendations for the Use of Compressed Air

Pupils must be taught to treat compressed air and pneumatic equipment with respect. Compressed air is stored energy. Air pressure on a piston in a cylinder can cause the piston to move at speed and produce a large force. Care should be taken to avoid fingers becoming trapped by moving piston rods. Secure pipe connections are essential, as a loose nylon pipe supplied at one end with live air from a valve can flail about in a violent and dangerous manner. Circuits should be thoroughly checked over for loose connections before being connected to the air supply.

Pupils must be warned of the dangers of playing pranks with compressed air. Compressed air introduced into the human body can kill. It should never be introduced into an orifice of the body, such as the mouth, ear or nose. Fingers should never be placed over pipes or valve ports from which compressed air is escaping, as there is a danger of an air bubble getting in the bloodstream, especially if there is an open cut in the skin. Eye protection and a dust mask should be used if compressed air is being used to clean dust, shavings or swarf from machinery with a blow gun. However, it is far better to use a vacuum cleaner for cleaning jobs.

Air Receiver Safety

Air receivers are pressure vessels. Great care must be taken to ensure that the receiver is of sound construction and has adequate strength. Use only commercially made air receivers which have been hydraulically tested, marked with a safe working pressure (SWP) and issued with a test certificate. *Never* use an improvised vessel, such as a Calor gas container, old oxygen gas cylinder or fire extinguisher as a receiver. A receiver, full of compressed air at high pressure, contains a tremendous amount of stored energy.

Example
What is the stored energy in an air receiver of size 400 mm diameter × 1000 mm long at pressure 10 bar?

Assuming the perfect gas law applies, the energy stored is given by

$$W = p_o V \log_e \frac{p_o}{p_a}$$ where p_o is the working pressure and p_a is the atmospheric pressure of 1 bar.

The interior volume of the receiver is

$$V = \frac{\pi}{4}(0.4)^2 \,(1.0) \text{ m}^3$$

$$= \frac{\pi}{4} \times 0.16 \times 1 \, m^3$$

$$= \pi \times 0.04 \times 1 \, m^3$$

therefore $V = 0.1254 \, m^3$.

1 bar is $1 \times 10^5 \, N \, m^{-2}$ so stored energy is

$$W = 10 \times 10^5 \times 0.125 \log_e \frac{10}{1} \, J$$

$$= 10^6 \times 0.125 \log_e 10 \, J$$

$$= 10^6 \times 0.125 \times 2.3026 \, J$$

therefore $W = 0.29 \times 10^6 \, J$.

Stored energy is $0.29 \times 10^6 \, J$ or $290 \, 000 \, J$.

It is interesting to calculate how high the receiver would have to be lifted off the ground so that its potential energy equalled the energy stored by the air inside it. The receiver's mass m is 160 kg.

$$mgh = 0.29 \times 10^6 \, J \text{ (where } h \text{ is height in metres)}$$

$$h = \frac{0.29 \times 10^6}{160 \times 9.8} \text{ metres (where the mass is 160 kg and } g = 9.8 \, m/s^2)$$

$$h = \frac{290 \, 000}{160 \times 9.8} \text{ metres}$$

$$= 179 \text{ metres.}$$

Receivers are usually cylindrical, although some pressure vessels are spherical. Very stringent rules control their design, construction and testing. The internal pressure causes stress in the walls of the receiver. In thin walled vessels, the stress in the cylindrical walls is given by the equations:

$$\sigma_1 = \frac{pr}{2t} \text{ (longitudinal stress, where } p \text{ is the pressure in the vessel,}$$

$$r \text{ is the mean radius and}$$

$$t \text{ is the wall thickness)}$$

$$\sigma_2 = \frac{pr}{t} \text{ (hoop or circumferential stress)}$$

Therefore $2\sigma_1 = \sigma_2$

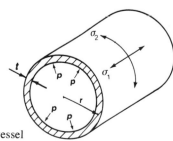

Fig. 5.1   Stress in a cylindrical pressure vessel

For a cylindrical pressure vessel, the circumferential stress is twice the longitudinal stress. So, if the pressure vessel cracks, it is likely that the crack will appear on the cylindrical surface of the vessel running longitudinally. (Think of a sausage splitting open!)

The minimum wall thickness is calculated from an equation given in BS 1515 (the British Standard covering design, materials, construction and testing of pressure vessels).

Wall thickness $t = \dfrac{pD_i}{2fJ - p}$ where p is the design pressure,

$\quad D_i$ is the internal diameter of the vessel,

$\quad J$ is the joint factor (usually 1.0 for radiographed welds) and

$\quad f$ is the design stress.

Pressure vessels are made of low carbon alloy steel as specified in BS 1515. They are arc welded and often given post welding heat treatment to relieve internal stresses. Non-destructive testing is carried out on welded joints. The pressure vessels are subjected to hydraulic pressure tests. A commercially manufactured air receiver has its safe working pressure (SWP) marked on a plate attached to the receiver. A test certificate is issued by the inspecting authority and two copies should be supplied when an air receiver is purchased.

Regular Inspection of Air Receivers

The inspection and testing of air receivers in service is covered by the Factories Act 1961, Section 36. The Act requires inspections to be made every twenty-six months by a competent engineer. The inspecting engineer is usually working on behalf of an insurance company. The air receiver must have an inspection port. The engineer will strike the receiver with a hammer and check for signs of internal corrosion. Hydraulic testing is also applied to the receiver and the fittings are inspected. Details of the inspection are recorded on a report form. This form is shown on the following pages.

The Factories Act 1961, Section 36, is now covered by the Health and Safety at Work Act 1974. Education Authorities should arrange for regular inspections of compressor units and air lines to be carried out by an engineer appointed by their insurance company. BS 4163, Section 5.9.7 (1975) Recommendations for Health and Safety in Workshops, Schools and Colleges suggests that air receivers should be inspected at least every two years.

Fig. 5.2 (opposite)   Specimen report form

Form containing prescribed particulars for

Report of Examination of Air Receiver

Notes

a If the receiver is installed in a factory, the name of the occupier should be given in **1**, and the address of the factory in **2**. If the receiver is in use in a temporary location, e.g. building operation, work of engineering construction, the address of the head office of the occupier should be given. If the receiver is in use in a ship registered in the United Kingdom (other than a fixed receiver permanently installed in a ship) the name of the owner of the receiver and the address of his head office should be given. Where the ship is registered outside the United Kingdom the name and address of the master or officer in charge of the ship should be given

b Items **5A, B** and **C** and certificate a should be completed except in the case of an examination under the Shipbuilding and Ship-repairing Regulations of

  (i) a receiver of solid drawn construction which cannot be throughly examined internally, when items **5B** and **D** and certificate b should be completed, or

  (ii) a receiver, other than described in (i) when items **5C** and certificate a should be completed

c According to the type of air receiver, facilities should be given by the occupier for such examination (internal and external), hammer testing, drilling, lifting, hydraulic testing, or other means of testing as may be necessary for the thorough examination

d Where, before furnishing replies to item 6, the person making the examination considers that further examination is necessary in order to test the fittings under normal pressure, a professional entry 'subject to supplementary report after examination under normal pressure' may be made in regard to the matters in question; provided that:

  (i) the thorough examination is completed within the statutory period and

  (ii) a supplementary report containing the prescribed particulars on form F60 is inserted in the General Register

1 Name of factory occupier or owner of air receiver (see note **a**)

2 Address (see note **a**)

3 Description and distinguishing mark of receiver and type

4 Date of construction (if ascertainable). The history should be briefly given, and the examiner should state whether he has seen the last previous report

Receiver (see note **b**)

5A What parts (if any) were inaccessible?

5B What examination and tests were made? (see note **c**)

5C Date of last hydraulic test   5D Pressure applied

5E Condition of receiver (state cleanliness of receiver and any defects materially affecting the safe working pressure)

External

Internal

Receiver

5F External condition (including cleanliness)

5G Hydraulic test pressure applied   5H Result of hydraulic test

Fittings

6A Are the required fittings and appliances provided in accordance with the Act?

6B Are all fittings and appliances properly maintained and in good condition? (see note **d**)

7 Repairs (if any) required and period within which they should be executed and any other condition which the person making the examination thinks it necessary to specify for securing safe working

F59 **To be inserted in the general register**

Continued overleaf

Notes continued

When the examiner considers that the next examination of a solid drawn receiver may be made after a period exceeding 26 months (in accordance with Section 36(4) (a) of the Factories Act 1961), the period within which the next examination is to be made should be specified in item 9

When the examiner considers it necessary he may insert in his report on any of the items 'subject to further report after examination under normal pressure'

Air receivers

Regulation 68 of the Shipbuilding and Ship-repairing Regulations 1960 applies the provisions of the Factories Act to air receivers other than fixed air receivers permanently installed in a ship

Section 36 of the Factories Act 1961 describes the fittings to be attached to an air receiver, the period for cleaning, and the period, manner and reporting of the examination and testing of air receivers.

8 Safe working pressure, calculated from dimensions and from the thickness and other data assertained by the present examination (due allowance being made for conditions of working if unusual or exceptionally severe)

Where repairs affecting the working pressure are required, state the safe working pressure:

8A before the expiration of the period specified in 7 overleaf

8B after the expiration of such period if the required repairs have not been completed

8C after the completion of the required repairs

9 Other observations (see note e)

Certification

a I certify that on
the air receiver described above was thoroughly clean and (so far as its construction permits) made accessible for thorough examination and for such tests as were necessary for thorough examination and that on the said date I thoroughly examined this receiver, including its fittings and that the above is a true report of my examination.

b I certify that on
I examined the air received described above and tested it hydraulically, and that the above is a true report of the results of my examination and test.

Signature

Qualification

Address

Date

If employed by a company or association give name and address

6 Project Briefs

Chapter 12 in the pupil text and Activity 12 deal with 'mini' projects. The time allocated for a mini project is two to four weeks, depending on the overall course length. It is highly unlikely that working and tested hardware can be produced by pupils in such a short time. What is possible is that pupils can produce a substantial design folder along with a bench test of an appropriate pneumatic circuit which would be incorporated in the hardware if it was built. Such an exercise would be an invaluable experience which prepares pupils for the design work associated with CSE and O-level major projects.

With regard to CSE and O-level major projects, any one of the ten mini project briefs given in Activity 12 would present a pupil with a substantial challenge. Considerable effort would be required if the end result was to be a finely engineered and well evaluated device.

A Bibliography

For Pupils' Use

Title	Author/Publisher	Comment
A Basic Guide to Pneumatic Circuitry	Schrader Bellows, Walkmill Lane, Bridgtown, Cannock, Staffordshire WS11 3LR	Slim A4 booklet. Good for ideas. Non BSI symbols.
Circuit Design	Maxam publication 208-70 from CompAir Maxam Ltd, Pool, Redruth, Cornwall TR15 3PR	Excellent booklet with good clear line diagrams.
Control Technology: Pupils' Assignments	Schools Council Project Technology EUP ISBN 0 340 18244 X	Very valuable parallel course to 'Modular Courses in Technology'. Some useful elementary circuits, but with confusion over the use of symbols (mixture of imperial and BSI/ISO symbols).
Control Technology: Follow-Up Sheets	Schools Council Project Technology EUP ISBN 0 340 18245 8	
Detection and Sensing with Air Jets	J. E. Graham Martonair Ltd, St Margaret's Road, Twickenham, Middlesex TWI IRJ	Excellent leaflet with many low pressure circuits and applications.
Instruction Manual for Fluidics Logic Experiments Kit	N. W. Sykes British Fluidics and Controls Ltd, Forest Road, Hainault, Ilford, Essex	Excellent booklet for teacher or pupil. Detailed information about fluidic logic and fluidic circuits.
Introducing Fluidics	Schools Council Project Technology Handbook No. 4 Heinemann Educational Books ISBN 0 435 75903 5	Booklet with some valuable application ideas. Components described are no longer available from supplier, but Norgren OR-NOR modules can be substituted.
Introduction to Digital Fluidics	IMI Norgren Ltd, Shipston-on-Stour, Warwickshire CV36 4PX	Excellent booklet for teacher and pupil use. Gives historical development of fluidics, some details about components and applications.
Guide to Air Control	Schrader Bellows	Slim A4 booklet. Excellent for ideas, illustrations and applications.
Guide to Practical Fluidic Circuits	IMI Norgren Ltd	Simple step-by-step guide to fluidic circuit design. Clear line diagrams.
Pneumatics at Work 1 Pneumatics at Work 2	Schrader Bellows	Slim A4 booklets. Illustrated industrial applications with text.

For Teacher's Use

Title	Author/Publisher	Comment
Control Technology: Teachers' Book	Schools Council Project Technology EUP ISBN 0 340 18243 1	Useful demonstration of pneumatic and fluidic circuits. Some homework examples for pupils. Confused mixture of symbols in circuits.
A Course in Applied Pneumatics	Martonair Ltd EDU/16200	Detailed course which is useful as reference book. Early chapters have some mathematics about air flow rates and forces. Good circuits in line drawing form, some applications.
Electronic Logic Circuits	J. R. Gibson Edward Arnold ISBN 0 7131 3407 0	A good introduction to logic systems, and fully compatible with their realisation with air operated equipment rather than electronic devices.
Fundamental Concepts	Unit 5 Open University Course PET 271 Technology for Teachers Open University Press ISBN 0335 02800 4	Excellent introduction to pneumatics. Many applications of pneumatic circuits at school level.
Journal of Applied Pneumatics	Martonair Ltd	Many articles on industrial pneumatics with industrial applications. Appears three times a year (April, August and December).
The Martonair Cascade System of Circuit Analysis	Martonair Ltd F6	Useful leaflet which outlines a method of designing circuits where complex sequences of cylinder movements are required.
Pneumatic Mechanization	F.S.G. Van Dijen Kemperman Technical Publishers ISBN 90 11 94150 0	English translation of book produced in Netherlands for training pneumatic engineers and technicians. Excellent book – the 'pneumatics bible'. Well illustrated with photos and line drawings. Basic principles, basic circuits and many applications are included.
Pneumatics Module	J. Whatley School Technology Forum National Centre for School Technology, Trent Polytechnic, Burton Street, Nottingham NG1 4BU	Syllabus guide and technological framework for pneumatics. A short concise booklet covering technology syllabus, pupil activities, objectives, teacher's notes, resources and hardware.

B Visual Aids

Pneumatics Filmstrip

A double-frame filmstrip has been produced to illustrate some aspects of the *Pneumatics* module. The filmstrip could be cut up, and each of the twenty-three frames mounted to form the basis of a slide collection to which the teacher can add over a period of time. The following notes refer to the frames on the filmstrip, which are numbered 1 to 23.

1   A large two-stage air compressor at Fanshawe School in Hertfordshire. The compressor is sited in its own specially built chamber outside the school building. It not only supplies air to the technology room for the pneumatics course, but also to metal and woodwork rooms for air powered tools. This arrangement makes optimum use of the compressed air facility and should be emulated wherever possible.

2   A modest compressed air facility. A small compressor is mounted on a vertical receiver. The unit is portable and pneumatic circuits are connected one at a time to a check unit to the left of the lubricator. The unit could be connected permanently to an air line with two or three check units, and it could operate several small pneumatic circuits simultaneously for a short time.

3   A close-up of the compressed air conditioning units seen in the previous picture. From right to left we see the filter, regulator with pressure gauge and then the lubricator. In the bottom right-hand corner the inspection hole plug, which when removed gives access to the interior of the air receiver, can be seen.

4   A more complex air conditioning system in a school technology room. Air from the compressor passes along the pipe on the left and is then filtered. The air line then divides. In the upper line, the air is regulated and lubricated, and is made available at check units round the room to power high pressure pneumatic equipment. In the lower line, the air is filtered again to improve its purity, and regulated to a low pressure to supply fluidic equipment at a number of check units round the room.

5   A sectioned Martonair double-acting, cushioned cylinder. Note the construction of the piston with its rubber seals and also the smaller diameter cushioning seals either side of the piston. Refer to Chapter 3 of the pupil text for details on cushioned cylinders, and see Fig. 3.9.

6   A sectioned Martonair mechanically operated, spring-returned 3-port spool valve. The spool valve is the simplest type of valve. The flow of air from the supply to the cylinder, or from the cylinder to exhaust, is controlled by the left/right movement of the three segmented spool and its rubber O-ring seals. Compare with Fig. 2.16 in the pupil text.

The remaining frames show various applications of pneumatics in a number of projects.

7   A pneumatically operated vice. The vice closes when the cylinders *instroke*. Discuss why the vice could apply a greater force if it was closed by the cylinders outstroking. Produce designs for such a system. Consider the problems of safety. Is speed control of the cylinders desirable in both directions? What if a user of the vice accidentally gets both hands trapped in it? Refer to Fig. 4.10 in the pupil text.

8   A combination lock system using air bleeds and diaphragm valves. Refer to Fig. 5.8 in the pupil text and compare the circuit shown there with this system. Discuss the weaknesses and strengths of these two solutions to the need for a combination lock system. Are there problems which neither solution solves? Can you evolve a specification for an 'ideal' combination lock? Can you then design it?

9   One answer to the need for a means by which the wear resistance properties of a fabric can be tested. Refer to Chapter 4 in the pupil text and consider the other options open to a designer attempting to meet this need.

10   A pneumatically operated vice and drill working together in a sequence of movements. Refer to Chapter 9 in the pupil text. Note the universal difficulty in keeping the pipework of school pneumatic projects neat and tidy!

11   A pneumatically operated barrier arm. A marriage of pneumatics and mechanisms in what, together with a good written report, could be an average CSE examination project. The model is quite nicely finished and is used to demonstrate a design idea for a solution to the need for a barrier arm when making a full size system is impractical.

12   Another solution to meet the need for a barrier arm. Compare this solution and the previous one with that shown in Fig. 6.7 of the pupil text. Try to work out the circuits shown in order to compare them with the circuit in Fig. 6.7. Appreciate that there is always more than one solution to a problem, and each solution has to be evaluated for its appropriateness in a particular circumstance.

13   The problem here was to devise a pneumatic system, controlled through a single joy stick, which would alter the attitude of a model aircraft according to the normally expected responses of an aircraft to joy stick control. Note that pneumatic cylinders move the whole aircraft and not its control surfaces, i.e. the ailerons and elevators. Design your own system.

14   When the push-button on the left is momentarily pressed, this machine dispenses sherry into the waiting glass! Study each part of this system. Draw up a block diagram of the system and try to evolve a diagram for the pneumatic circuit. The equipment in the background is a small air compressor with a low voltage motor supplied by a transformer. This equipment allows the system to be strategically sited in the headmaster's study!

15 and 16   Two views of a drawer testing machine designed to evaluate the wear resistance properties of the runners. Reciprocation of the cylinder continuously opens and closes the drawer. Note the weights inside the drawer which load its runners. Consider the various types of circuit which can cause a cylinder to reciprocate. Refer to Fig. 7.14 in the pupil text. Discuss how the number of drawer movements could be counted.

17 and 18   The previous pictures showed pupil projects. These two show an industrial project in which a pneumatically operated rig tests mass-produced steel and plastic chairs. The chair is repeatedly 'sat on' until a component fails. Instruments record the applied loads on the seat and the chair back, the deflection of parts of the chair structure, and the total number of times the chair has been 'sat on'. Discuss the ways a chair structure is loaded by persons of different weights and sizes. Discuss the effect on a chair's structure of, for example, sitting on it tipped back with the rear legs taking all the load.

19 and 20   Compressed air and pneumatic equipment can be immensely useful in school workshops. These two frames show a fly press in which the usual screw and weights have been replaced by a very large (in bore and stroke) pneumatic cylinder which was surplus to the requirements of a local company. A very large range of press tools and punches can be operated by this press. Discuss why the pneumatic system is much safer than the conventional screw and weights fly press.

21 and 22   Still in the school workshops, an injection moulding machine's ram is operated by a pneumatic cylinder. Note the second order lever to which the cylinder is attached. Is the load force greater or smaller than the force applied by the cylinder? Note also the link at the top of the lever. Discuss why the link is needed here rather than a rigid fulcrum point for the lever. Why is the cylinder mounted, at its rear, on a trunnion rather than rigidly fixed to the square tube base frame? Discuss injection moulding of plastics.

23   No matter how limited a school's pneumatic equipment is initially, the supply will soon be extended by acquisitions from local industries. One use for large bore and long stroke cylinders is a rig such as this which will dramatically demonstrate the very large forces pneumatic cylinders can generate. The heaviest pupil in the class (perhaps even several heavy pupils) can be lifted high in the air with absolute ease at the touch of a button. Get pupils to work out the bore diameter of the pneumatic cylinder which would just lift them. Stipulate the pressure of the compressed air supply. See Chapter 2 of the pupil text.

Martonair Overhead Projection Foil Set (EDU/22324)

This set consists of twenty-four multi-coloured foils with accompanying text. Included are single-acting and double-acting cylinders, 3-port and 5-port valves, a sectioned flow regulator, etc.

Masters for Overhead Projector Transparencies

Teachers may find the following OHP masters useful for illustrating pneumatics theory lessons. They can either be traced manually with suitable master pens directly on to OHP transparency sheets, or they can be used with an OHP master-making machine which will give a facsimile reproduction on the transparent sheet of the master. When making up transparencies showing the more complex circuits, it is recommended that a layering technique be used in which several transparencies are used for different parts of the circuit. When projected, pupils can then be shown the circuit being built up in a number of simple stages, starting with pure component symbols and ending with the completed circuit. Such layered visual aids must be prepared by hand drawing methods, and it is recommended that different coloured pens are used to enhance their impact.

Pneumatic Devices

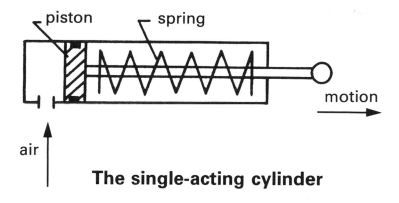

The single-acting cylinder

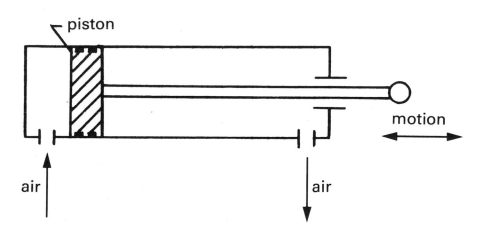

The double acting-cylinder

2   The 3-port Valve

Without button pressed

With button pressed

Complete symbol

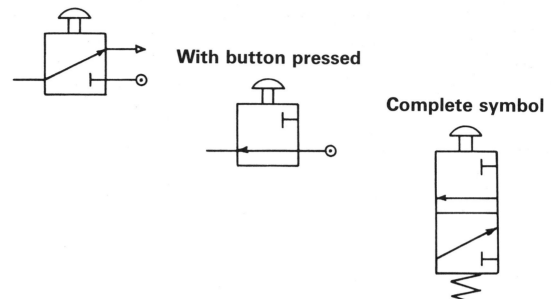

The push-button operated, spring-return 3-port valve

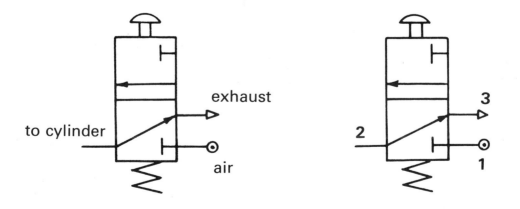

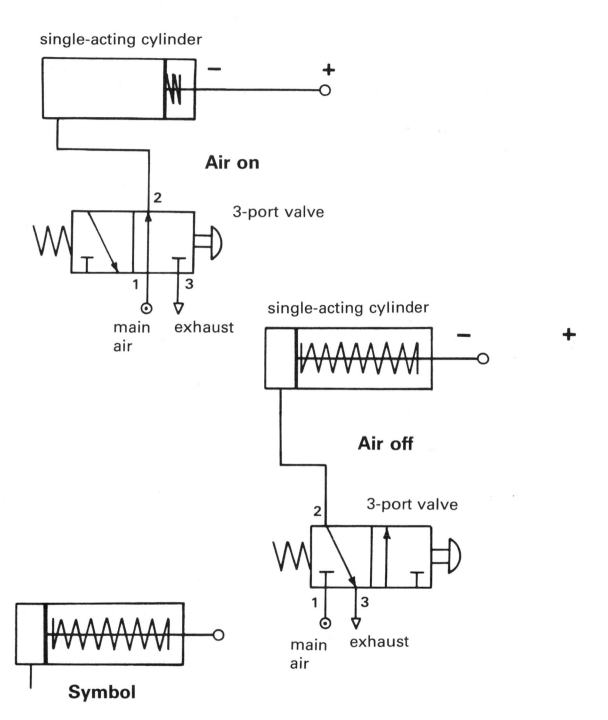

single-acting cylinder

Air on

2

3-port valve

1   3

main
air   exhaust

single-acting cylinder

Air off

2   3-port valve

1   3

main
air   exhaust

Symbol

Lever set/reset operated

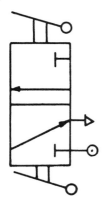

Push-button operated

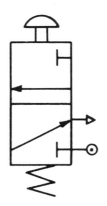

Roller-trip operated

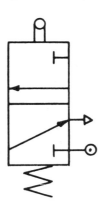

Foot-pedal operated

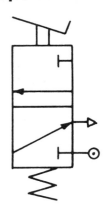

Plunger operated

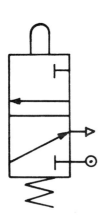

Signal air operated

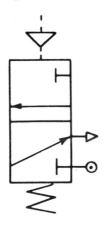

Diaphragm operated

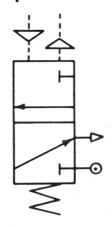

Solenoid operated

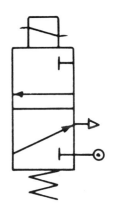

5   3-port Valve Control of a Double-acting Cylinder

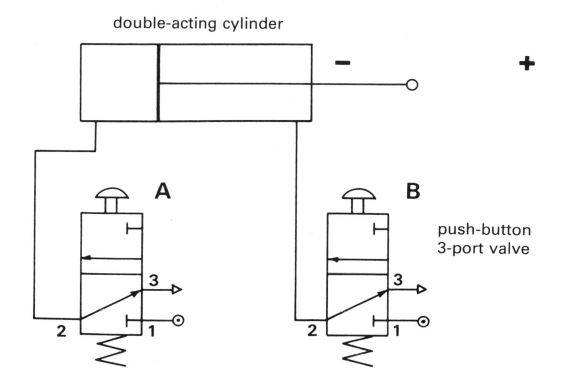

double-acting cylinder

A

B

push-button
3-port valve

The 5-port Valve (Lever Set/Reset)

Symbol

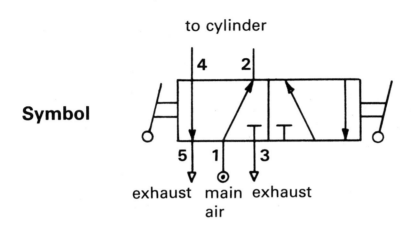

to cylinder

4 2

5 1 3

exhaust main exhaust
air

7 5-port Valve Control of a Double-acting Cylinder

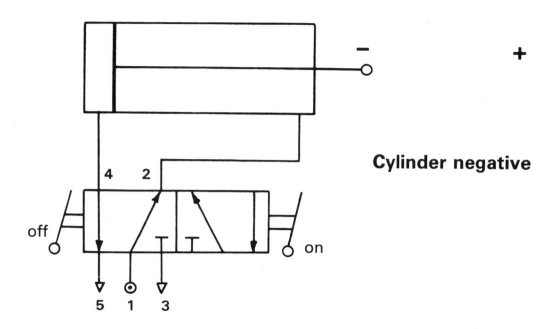

Cylinder negative

4   2

off

5   1   3

on

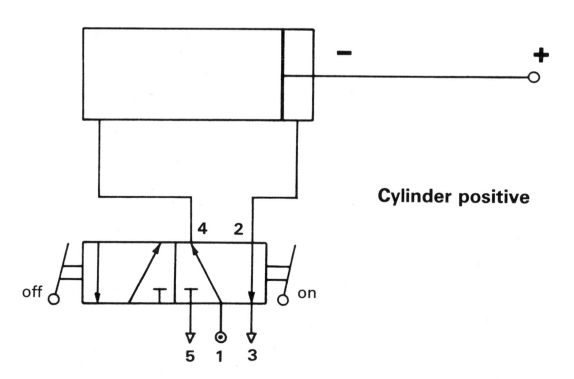

Cylinder positive

4   2

off

on

5   1   3

8 The Double Pressure Operated 5-port Valve

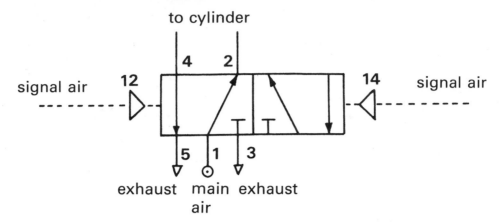

to cylinder

4   2

signal air   12   14   signal air

5 1 3

exhaust   main exhaust
          air

Pilot 3-port Valve Control of a Double-acting Cylinder

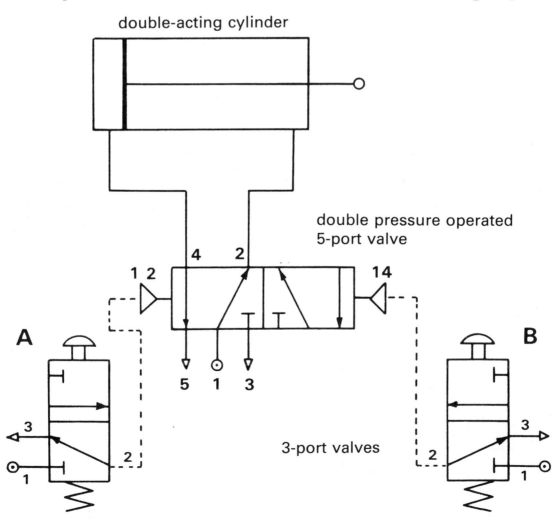

double-acting cylinder

double pressure operated
5-port valve

4   2

1 2   14

A   B

5 1 3

3   3

3-port valves

2   2

1   1

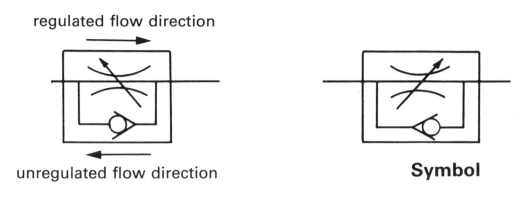

regulated flow direction

unregulated flow direction

Symbol

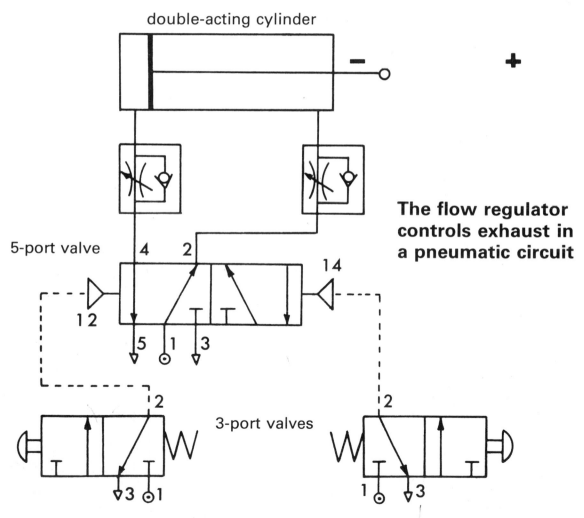

double-acting cylinder

The flow regulator controls exhaust in a pneumatic circuit

5-port valve

3-port valves

Air Bleed Control of a Double-acting Cylinder

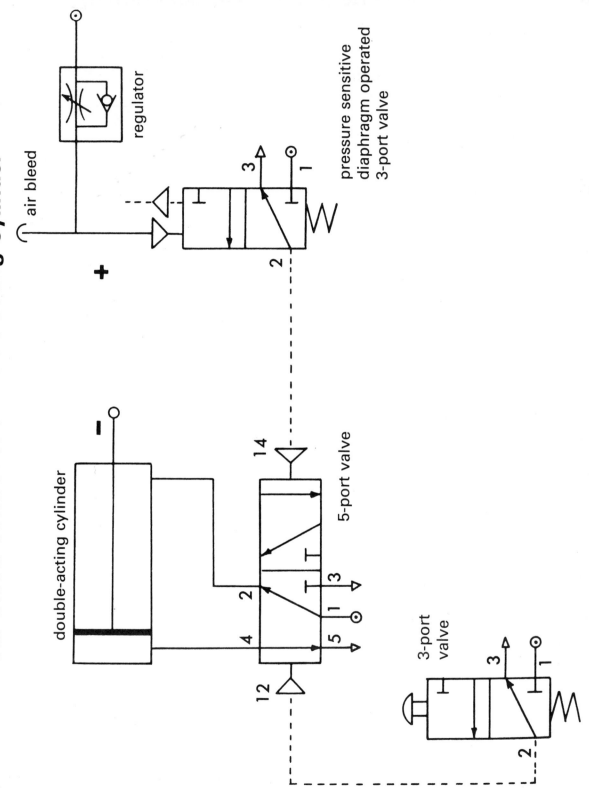

regulator

air bleed

+

pressure sensitive
diaphragm operated
3-port valve

3

1

2

double-acting cylinder

14

5-port valve

2

3

1

4

5

12

3-port
valve

3

1

2

Solenoid Valve Control of a Pneumatic Cylinder

11

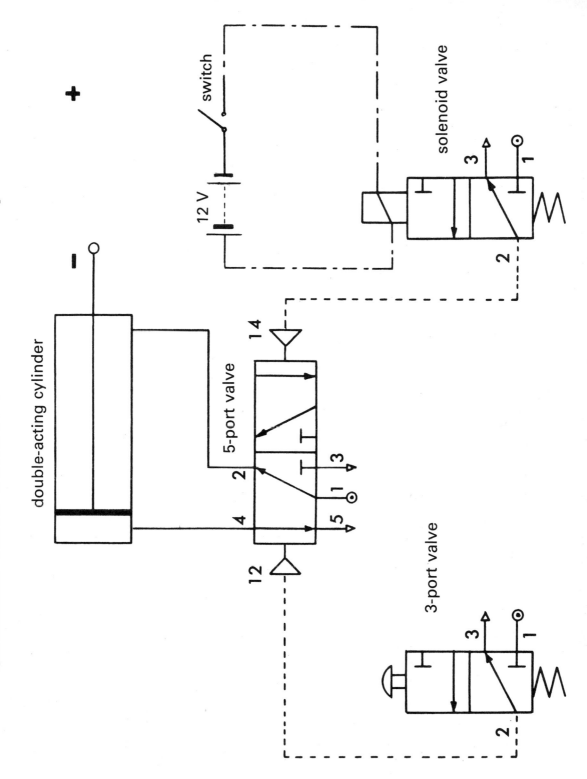

switch

12 V

+

−

double-acting cylinder

solenoid valve

5-port valve

14

2

3

1

4

5

12

3-port valve

3

1

2

Automatic Control of a Cylinder

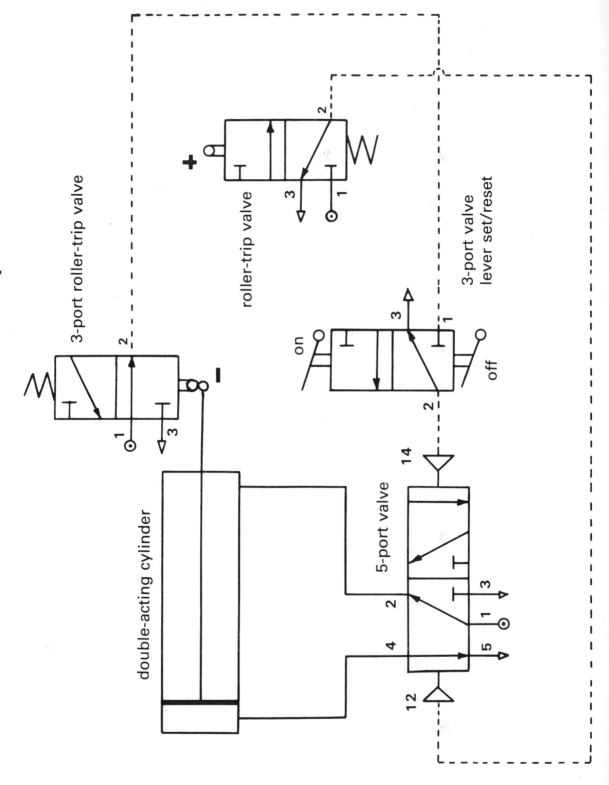

3-port roller-trip valve

roller-trip valve

3-port valve
lever set/reset

double-acting cylinder

5-port valve

13

Time Delay in Controlling a Pneumatic Cylinder

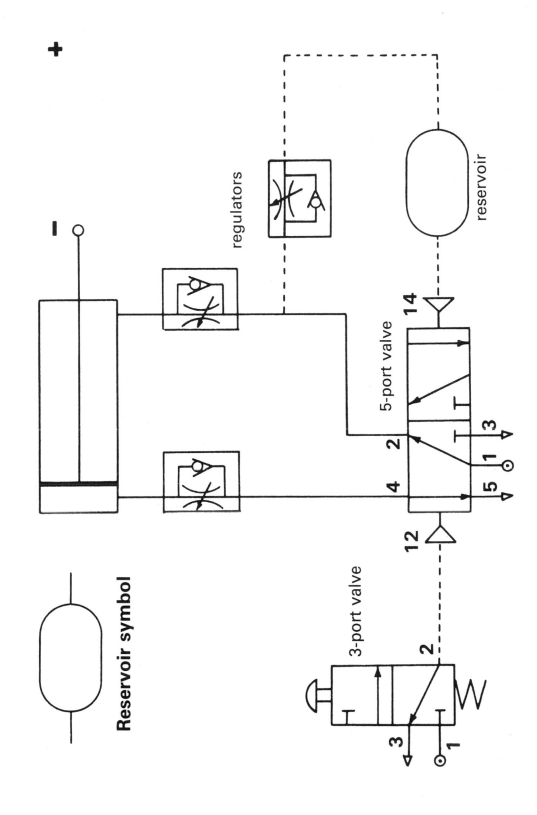

Reservoir symbol

regulators

reservoir

5-port valve

3-port valve

Time Delay to Produce an Automatic Pneumatic Circuit

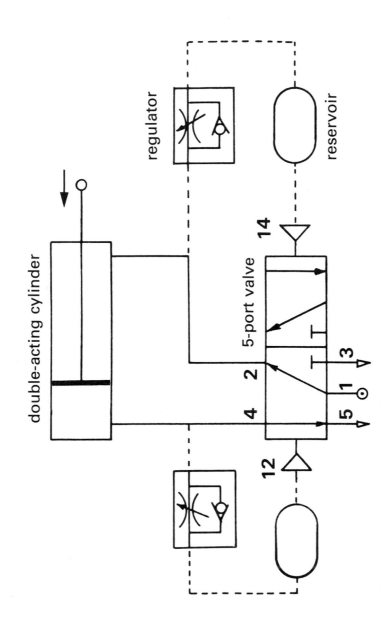

double-acting cylinder

regulator

reservoir

5-port valve

12

14

2

4

3

1

5

Sequential Control of Two Cylinders 1

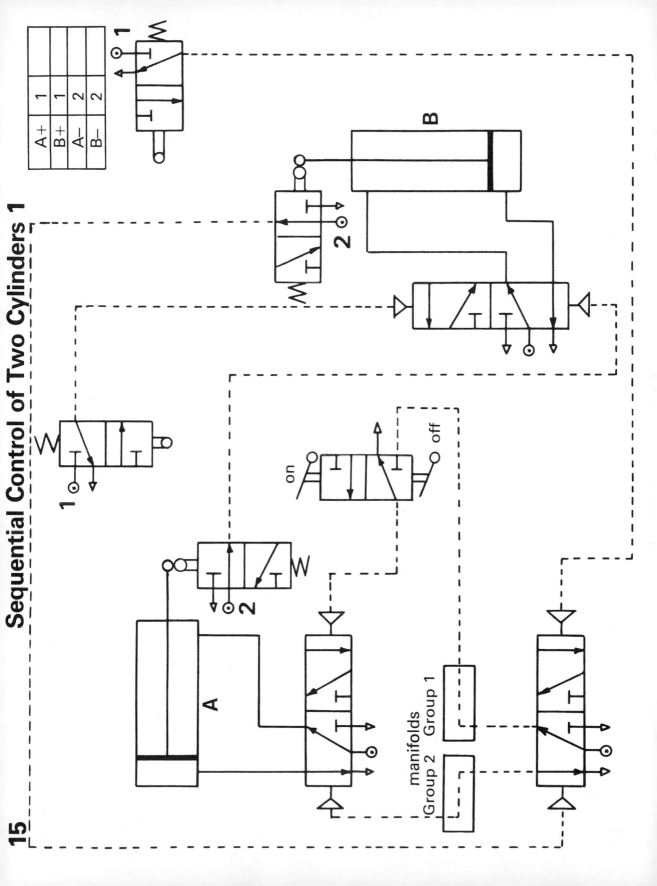

A+	1
B+	1
A−	2
B−	2

manifolds
Group 2 Group 1

on   off

15

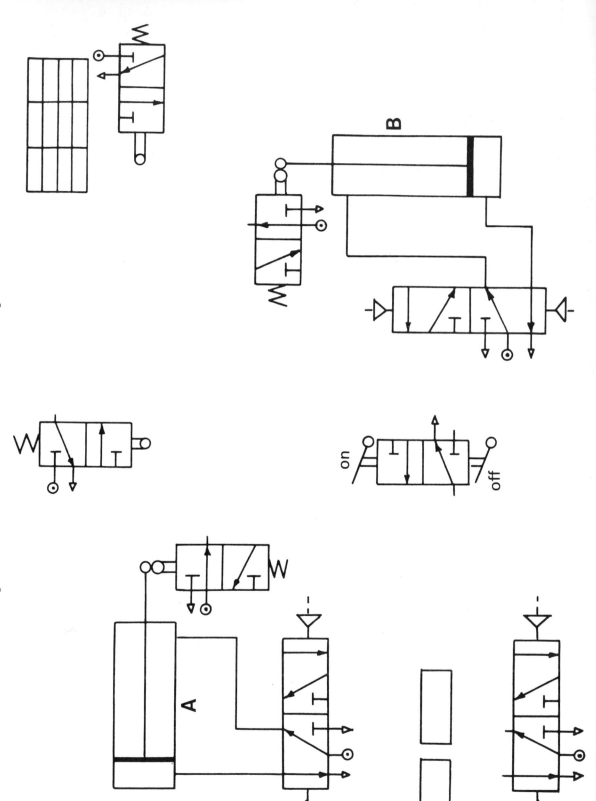

Sequential Control of Three Cylinders

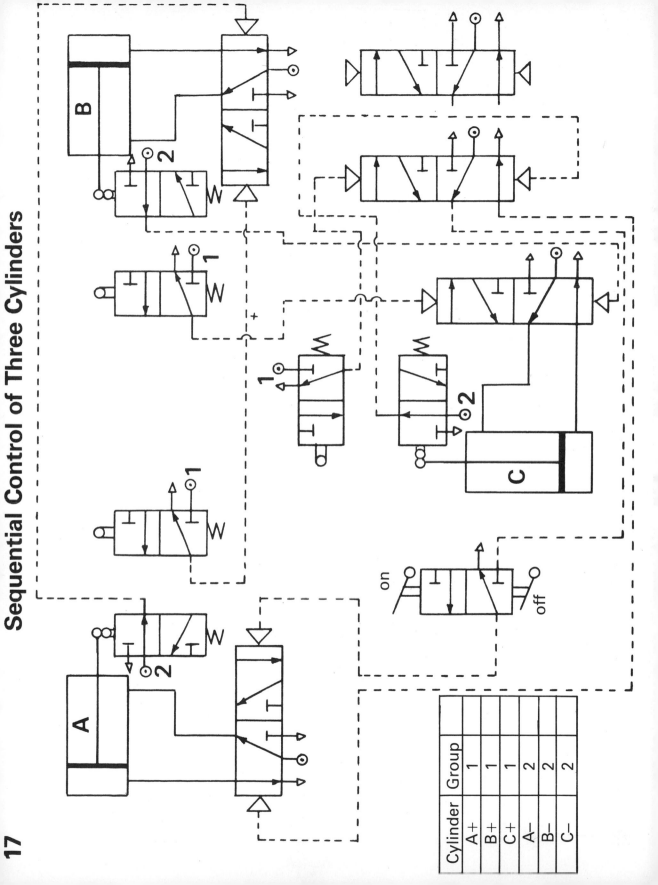

Cylinder	Group
A+	1
B+	1
C+	1
A–	2
B–	2
C–	2

C Useful Addresses

Pneumatic Components

CompAir Maxam Ltd, Pool, Redruth, Cornwall TR15 3PR. Tel: Redruth (0209) 712712.

Economatics Ltd, 4 Orgreave Crescent, Dore House Industrial Estate, Handsworth, Sheffield S13 9NQ Tel: Sheffield (0742) 690801.

Enots Ltd, PO Box 22, Eastern Avenue, Lichfield, Staffordshire WS13 6SB. Tel: Lichfield 54151.

IMI Norgren Ltd, Shipston-on-Stour, Warwickshire CV36 4PX. Tel: Shipston-on-Stour (0608) 61676.

Kay Pneumatics, Half Moon Hill, London Road, Dunstable, Bedfordshire. Tel: Dunstable (0582) 609292.

Martonair Ltd, St Margaret's Road, Twickenham, Middlesex TW1 1RJ. Tel: 01-892 4411.

Schrader Bellows, Walkmill Lane, Bridgtown, Cannock, Staffordshire WS11 3LR. Tel: Cannock 2644.

Fluidic Components and Low Pressure Devices

British Fluidics and Controls Ltd, Forest Road, Hainault, Ilford, Essex. Tel: 01-500 3300.

CompAir Maxam, Economatics, Enots, IMI Norgren, Kay Pneumatics and Martonair – addresses given above.

Compressors and Air Line Equipment

BroomWade compressors from: CompAir Industrial Ltd, PO Box 7, BroomWade Works, High Wycombe, Buckinghamshire HP13 5SF. Tel: High Wycombe (0494) 21181.

Clarkes economy range of compressors from: The Clarke Group, Lower Clapton Road, Hackney, London E5 ORN. Tel: 01-986 8231.

Economatics – address given above.

Many firms have a minimum order charge. This can make it difficult for a school to obtain single items or small quantities. To help schools, Economatics have no minimum order charge, but for small orders require cash with order plus a postage and packing charge. Enquiry should be made of the prevailing terms of business before placing an order. Other suppliers may be willing to do business on a similar basis.